Think Conceptually, Act Procedurally

◆

Think Conceptually, Act Procedurally

Understanding the difference between thinking and learning concepts and procedures.

◆

Jerry E. Carney

Writers Club Press
San Jose New York Lincoln Shanghai

Think Conceptually, Act Procedurally
Understanding the difference between thinking and
learning concepts and procedures.

Writers Club Press
an imprint of iUniverse.com, Inc.

For information address:
iUniverse.com, Inc.
5220 S 16th, Ste. 200
Lincoln, NE 68512
www.iuniverse.com

ISBN: 0-595-20134-2

Printed in the United States of America

Contents

———————— ◆ ————————

Foreword

◆

The only thing that we own is the knowledge that we possess. No one can take your knowledge away from you. However, you can given it away as many times as you want. When you die, it dies with you if you haven't shared it with others. People possess many type of knowledge. They know the rules and procedures for doing things such as the rule that two plus two equals four. They also possess much knowledge about concepts or ideas. The two types of knowledge are complementary. Rules and procedures are developed to standardize and institutionalize the knowledge of concepts and ideas.

Knowledge is different than material possessions. With a material object when it is given to someone else, the person who gives it no longer owns it. Only a single person can possessed it at a time. However, knowledge can be shared with others without losing possession of it. Therefore, one should expect that both types of knowledge should be shared in the same frequency and with the same willingness. However, I have observed in my work experience and personal life that the two type of knowledge are not shared equally. People's willingness to share knowledge is related to do their personal values, personality, and style of learning among other factors. These reasons will be discussed in this book.

The information and ideas in this book are based on my experience. I have not performed any rigorous scientific experiments to verify these ideas. I have some thoughts about how some of these ideas could be tested but I believe that the ideas are simple enough that the reader can judge for themselves the value of the ideas.

Many books have been written about and many studies have been made about people personalities and how they think, interact with other people, etc. There are similarities between some of these ideas and what I will be proposing in this book. It is not my intent to point out the similarities or differences. If the reader is familiar with any of these, then they can make the comparisons for themselves. Let me say that I think that all of these ideas miss a fundamental issue that people acquire, process, and distribute information differently. This different is fundamental to humans and it has many consequences that will be discussed in this book.

Introduction

◆

There is a saying "To err is human, to really foul-up you need a computer". A computer can replicate the same error with great speed. A computer can add 2 to every number in the file but it can subtract 2 just as easily. An example where the computer could replicate a single error into many errors would be where the interest rate was entered wrong into a program that calculates the amount due on a loan. The human error is to put the wrong amount into the computer that is one error. The computer can then replicate this single error to thousands of loans within seconds.

The saying above misses an important point. Errors that a computer makes are simple. They are simple in the sense that they represent errors that are easily recognized and corrected. In the above example every loan would be wrong and would be easier to identify this type of error than an error that occurs only occasionally. They are also simple in that anyone no matter how knowledgeable they are about the loan system could make a mistake when inputting an interest rate. There is a different type of error: the errors caused by a lack of understanding.

The first type of error is caused when a person knows what to do but makes a mistake. In the loan system sample if the person who is entering a new interest rate presses the seven key instead of the eight key, then the system will calculate the wrong amount due for each loan. Each loan will be charged less interest than is due. This type of error is simple in two ways. The first way is that it is easier to recognize. The person who made the mistake is likely to recognize it immediately or the checks and balances that are normally built into business processes will catch it. Secondly, once the error has been recognized, it can be easily correctly by the computer.

The second type of error is caused when the person who enters or calculates the premium on the loan does not thoroughly understand their responsibilities. Most banks base the interest rates that they charge on the prime rate. The prime rate is the interest rate that bank borrow money from the Federal Reserve System. A bank will then mark this rate up to cover their costs and provide their profits. The amount that the prime rate is marked up will be determined by many factors such as the credit worthiness of the borrower and the amount of collateral. This makes the calculation of the interest rate to be charged an individual borrower a subjective matter. The subjective nature of the decision opens the door for the second type of error. These errors occur because of the lack of knowledge and are more difficult to identify and correct.

This second type of error is caused by a lack of knowledge. However, it is not just any type of knowledge. It is the knowledge of concepts and ideas. A person may know all of the procedures and all of the rules but if they don't understand the concepts and ideas, they can still make errors of the second kind. Knowledge of concepts and ideas allows people to develop new rules to meet new conditions or to apply their existing rules/knowledge to new or changing environments. It is the difference between knowing rules to follow and understanding the concepts that generated the rules in the first place.

The two types of errors have different causes. The first is incomplete procedures or a failure to follow the procedures carefully or a simple human error and the second is caused by a lack of conceptual understanding. This book could be described as a book about these two types of knowledge: the knowledge of procedures and the knowledge of concepts. This book will attempt to show that people vary in their ability to learn and communicate these two types of knowledge. This book will discuss some of the reasons for these differences. In addition, this book will investigate how procedural knowledge and conceptual knowledge differ, how the difference effects our ability to compete in an increasingly complex world, and the problems which we face in trying to teach or communicate procedures or concepts, and the power of each.

Only knowledge of the concepts can be applied to new situation, knowledge of directions can not be applied to new situations. Only concepts (ideas) can be molded and stretched to cover new and exciting situations. Specific directions can only be applied to a specific situation. To unlock the true potential of the human mind people must be allowed and encouraged to learn new ideas and to understand why they do things and why their procedures work. Our companies, schools, government bodies must instill an atmosphere where people are encouraged to question and learn not to just follow directions.

Before delving into the intricacies of procedures and concepts and how they relate to people, we need to consider a few examples of the procedures versus concepts. The hope is that the reader will get a feel for the differences between the two. This book will probably emphasize the conceptual aspects of knowledge more than the rules based portion of knowledge. From personal experience society does not place enough emphasis on learning concepts. This should not create the impression that rules based knowledge is any less important. Both types of knowledge are important. Most successful individuals in this world are very adept at learning and exercising both types of knowledge. They are able to recognize when to utilize each type of ability. Some situations require the application of procedures and others require an understanding of the concepts and ideas.

What is a concept or idea? Formulating an answer to this question, demonstrates one of the reasons that rules are emphasized over ideas in society. It is difficult to put into words what a concept or idea is. Rather than try to define a concept or idea, lets discuss some examples. In a cartoon when the cartoonist draws a light bulb above a character's head, the cartoonist is trying to show us that the character has just come up with an idea. Most people can relate to this kind of experience. This occurs when a person suddenly understand how to fix a problem that they have not been able to solve before. They have not identified all of the detailed steps required to solve it but they are still sure that their solution will work. In a high school geometry class a concept or idea would be equivalent to the knowledge of how to solve a problem (knowing which theorem(s) to use) and the rules would be the complete set of steps needed to formalize the solution and communicate it to others. A person may know how to solve the problem and still have difficulty in identifying the proper step to prove it. Likewise, a person may be able to work through a correct solution by following a process without possessing any real understanding of why the process produces a solution. When studying a new subject, the light bulb represents the fact that the underlying concepts of the subject have been learned.

Cooking provides another example that everyone should be able to relate to. There is a difference in the knowledge that is required to prepare a meal and to develop a new dish. There is a certain knowledge and expertise required to follow a recipe. This knowledge and expertise might be very valuable in a large restaurant where the same recipe must be executed consistently over and over again in order for the restaurant to be successful. The ability to teach others and manage others in the preparation of the recipe would also be important. However, this type of knowledge and expertise will not help if the restaurant needs to develop a different and distinctive new cuisine. This will require a chef who has a deep understanding of how certain flavors interact, what cooking processes can be adapted to the restaurant's kitchen, etc. This type of chef will be able to develop new recipes because he understands the concepts and ideas that determine the taste, smell, and look of foods. Both types of knowledge are important. The knowledge of the food preparation is important for the daily operation of the restaurant.

The knowledge of how to develop new recipes is important if people have become tired of the current menu of the restaurant.

Since the world is changing so rapidly, it is imperative for all organization to maintain the type of knowledge that allows the organization to respond to changes. Any set of rules (a recipe) is bound to become obsolete quickly. Today, restaurants must change their cuisine rapidly to maintain the interest of the general public. Only an understanding of concepts provides the knowledge to adjust rules or recipes to changing situations. Without this understanding disastrous errors will be made when a set of rules or recipe is changed. However, in order for modern society to benefit from new ideas and concepts, the knowledge must be turn into a set of rules so that it can be quickly taught to others and used by everyone.

Individuals lack an understanding of concepts for three main reasons. The first is that they have been taught rules and not concepts. It is common in business today to only teach a new employee the rules that he (she) needs to follow. They are not given any understanding of why the rules work. The second reason is that many people only want to learn the rules. They are anxious to get started and they only want to learn the rules. It is easier to learn some rules or to follow a set of procedures than it is to understand the underlying ideas of the process. The third reason is that they have developed an understanding but this understanding is wrong. Every individual will develop their own concepts and ideas to support the rules that they have learned. This is part of the process of organizing the information in our brains. The idea or concept may be very simple such as that there is no reason for the rules. It doesn't matter how simple or inaccurate the idea is. Every individual develop some kind of idea to support the rules that they are following.

The first two of these three reasons causes an incorrect understanding. If people were taught or were given the time to learn the true concepts which justify what they are doing, then people would not have to develop their own concepts which may be incorrect. Anyone who understands the concepts of an internal combustion engine appreciates the requirement that the engine oil level be maintained. A person does not have to be able to change the oil or even know how to add oil to understand how important it is that the engine oil level be maintained at a satisfactory level. No amount of instruction on how to change and add oil will ever teach anyone how important the oil is to the engine. Only when the person understands what oil does in the engine, will he be conscientious in maintaining it. In a similar manner before substituting ingredients in a food recipe, a thorough understanding of what each ingredient does in the recipe is needed. When substituting one ingredient for another, the differences in flavor, texture and how it combines with the other ingredients are all-important factors that will need to be considered. A person who does not understand all of these factors may believe that a simple substitution such as whole cream for milk can be made in any recipe if they saw that the substitution was allowed in one recipe.

The next section will develop in detail the difference between knowledge of procedures and knowledge of the concepts. It deals with addition. This is something that everyone should be familiar with. The rules of addition allow a person to add 221 to 109 by the following steps.

1. Add 9 and 1 to get 10.
2. Write the 0 of the result 10 in the answer and carry the one to the next column.
3. Add 2 and 0 plus the one that was carried to get 3.
4. Write 3 in the answer and carry nothing to the next column since 3 is less than 10.
5. Add 2 and 1 to get 3.
6. Write 3 in the answer.
7. The answer is 330.

These basic steps can be applied to any two numbers no matter how big the numbers. Most individuals have no trouble applying these rules and perform them easily and efficiently.

The arithmetic that we learn in elementary school is founded on using a base 10 numbering system. For this reason most people would say that it is easy to add 1 and 9 in our base 10 numbering system with the Arabic representation. Most people have more difficulty in adding I plus IX which is the same problem written in Roman numerals. They have even more difficulty if you ask them to add 1 to 1001 where the numbers are binary representations (This is the same problem in binary). The person who has difficulty adding two binary numbers does not understand the concepts that make the addition of two numbers 1 and 9 so easy. This person has knowledge of the rules but not the concepts upon which the number system that we are familiar with is based. A person who does not understand the concepts of number representation might believe that our base 10 numbering system is unique and that any other system is more difficult. He might believe that there is something important about using 10 for our numbering system. However, it is the Arabic numerals with positional representation that makes our numbering system simple and positional representation can be used with any base other than 10.

When people misunderstand what the underlying concepts are or assign the wrong importance to the concepts, then they are unable to effectively apply those concepts to new and different situations. Many people have difficulty applying the concepts that are embodied in the rules that they learn in elementary school to the problem of different numbering systems. Our arithmetic rules work just as easily in other numbering systems if the Arabic representation system is used.

As an example when we add to binary numbers such as 11100011 and 111011. We can use the same rules as when adding two based ten numbers such as 123490 and 2398.

$$
\begin{array}{ll}
11100011 & 123490 \\
\underline{+111011} & \underline{+2398} \\
100011110 & 125888
\end{array}
$$

We carry 1 to the next column when the sum of the two numbers is larger than the base. In the case of the binary number you carry when you reach 2. This is a lot simpler than trying to add two Roman numeral system numbers such as

MCIII

+LIII

MLCVI

The rules for adding Roman numerals are much more complex and harder to apply. This is true even though Roman numerals are a representation of base 10 numbers. It is simple to apply the rules of Arabic representation to another numbering system such as the binary example and perform addition or subtraction. The person may not have an intuitive feel for how large or small the numbers are but a person can still perform addition or subtraction with them.

A person who has a firm grasp of the concepts of the Arabic numbering system should be able to readily transfer the knowledge of how to perform addition and subtraction from the base ten system to other numbering systems based on other integers. Many people are not able to transfer the rules of performing simple arithmetic to new situations because they only have learned the rules and have not learned the underlying concepts. Since the mind needs some concept to relate the rules to, their minds will rationalize that the important concept which makes the rules work is the fact that they are working with a base 10 system. This makes it even more difficult to apply their knowledge to new situations.

When people don't understand the concepts or don't understand the relative importance of the concepts, they are not able to apply them to new situations. They are also doomed to make catastrophic mistakes. Mistakes of this type are more troublesome than computer mistakes because they are more difficult to identify and correct. These errors are difficult to identify because they are not recognized as errors. Until there is an understanding of why you are doing something, you are bound to keep repeating the same error.

The human mind is superior to the fastest computer not in its ability to follow detailed instructions but its ability to understand complex processes at a very general level and then apply that knowledge (understanding) to new situations. The changes that a person goes through as they mature or they grow old are very complex. They can profoundly change the appearance of a person. However, we are still able to recognize someone that we have not seen them for many years. People accurately apply a general understanding (how people age and how their appearance changes) to a specific situation. For a computer to perform this task would require years of efforts to define the specific rules for comparing two pictures of a person to determine if the pictures are of the same person at different ages.

Another example of the power of concepts would be chess. The first chess programs that were developed had a specific set of criteria for evaluating (rating) each possible current move plus a finite number of future moves. The chess program would then choose as its next move that move which had the highest rating. A chess master will evaluate fewer possible current and future moves. He will instead be more concerned with developing a defensive position or offensive position than in each individual move. A person will never be successful playing chess like a computer analyzing each current move and future move. The only way for a person to be successful is to learn the concepts of how to defend his own king and how to attack the opponent's king. The human brain is not designed to analyze millions of possibilities to determine the best. It is designed to recognize patterns.

In today's complex world it is difficult to spend the time to teach concepts. People would rather teach rules because it is easier to teach rules than ideas. It is difficult and time consuming to explain concepts and ideas. The demands of our technical society require people to learn more and more each day so we take shortcuts in school and industry.

People are only taught what they will need to know. This solves an immediate problem and allows people to function effectively in society. However, the individual and society will lose in the future because these individuals will not be as effective as they should be.

If humans think and act on concepts, then why is this book needed when concepts are so natural? The problem is that concepts are not taught in school, industry, etc. People are taught the how to do task and are not taught the why. Society has done a remarkable job of getting people to ignore their natural instincts. This process starts early before children are even in school. This is reinforced by the need to produce immediate results throughout school and in people's working career. There is so much pressure for results that it is a miracle that anyone ever asks why.

Human have a need for order and for the assurance of definite results. Humans have a need to know that if A, B, and C are performed; then D will occur. Rules provide boundaries that give structure and stability to our lives. Change and surprise can provide exhilaration and keep people motivated and stimulated but humans still need stability in their lives. There is a lot of comfort in knowing that certain actions generate a specific result. For this reason rules and procedures have a certain appeal to all people. They are like a security blank that a person can pull over himself and hide from the world.

A third reason for a re-evaluation is that some people have a different orientation to learning. Some are satisfied with rules while others have a real need to understand. The need to understand varies between people. Some people have a stronger need to understand than others. People approach work and learning in different ways. It is important to understand the differences between people and how they learn. People's style of learning is just as important to the learning process as is the language that the person speaks. If a person does not speak English, then they will learn very little from a course that is taught in English only. Our education processes need to be aware of these differences just as schools make adjustments for students that speaks another language.

Finally, society needs to emphasize concepts because when people don't understand the concept that controls a process, they are bound to commit errors of understanding. In today's world people are learning rules and procedures without understanding the concepts all of the time. It happens in the classrooms across the country when teachers instruct their students in the rules of grammar or mathematics and don't spent sufficient time on the concepts. It happens on the factory floor when managers try to implement the practices of Japanese companies but don't implement the concepts of partnership, less class distinction, and greater teamwork without which the practices are bound to fail.

There are many reasons why people do not gain a deep understanding of underlying concepts. Unless people learn to deal with these causes, they are doomed to continually commit the same errors. This book will provide some insight into what causes this lack of understanding and how to increase this understanding. The rest of the book will investigate the different types of people, how people learn, concepts in business, failures to understand concepts, misconceptions and future changes.

Lessons of History

◆

Studying history can help to predict and deal with the future. One of the most important lessons of history is that change is inevitable. People need to recognize and understand how these changes will affect society and their personal lives. Just because people are satisfied with their current jobs, family life, etc. does not mean that they can isolate themselves from the changes that are occurring around them. The world is changing at an amazing pace. This affects all aspects of life. Though, a person may love his or her job and be happy to work at it the rest of their life, that job may not exist in the future. Technological changes are eliminating the need for many types of jobs all the time. History shows any number of jobs that have been eliminated by change such as the telephone switchboard operator, etc.

In order to understanding and apply the lessons of history to the present and future people must understand the concepts and ideas that have shaped history and the concepts and ideas that apply in the present. They must also be able to recognize the changes that are just starting to make their presence felt in our lives. The lessons of history to be learned are not the date and facts but the ideas and concepts. If people only learn the dates and battles of the Revolutionary and Civil War, then they will miss the ideas and concepts that can help them with the present. Too often people learn the facts about history but lose sight of the important ideas that were important to the course of history. The reasons why any war occurs and what events lead to the conflict are more important than the dates and places of the battles. However, people are more likely to remember the dates and places of the battles and the important ideas.

Memorizing dates and places will not help anyone to recognize or deal with a divisive issue such as slavery was in the nineteenth century United States. Yet the world is faced with many issues that are just as divisive today. Arab and Jewish conflict in the Middle East and Catholics and Protestants in Northern Ireland are just a couple of examples. There are many more to choose from. The ability to name the dates and the places that are important to Muslims, Jews, Protestants or Catholics will not further the cause of peace in any area of the world even if it is Protestants who know about Catholics dates and places or Muslims who know about Jewish dates and places. Now if a Protestant would learn and understand why the Catholics feel that it is so important that Northern Ireland be united with the rest of Ireland and the Catholics reciprocate, then real progress can be made.

The lessons of history are available to everyone but they are often painful to accept. People would rather bury their heads in the ground than to face the realities of their situation. In order to learn from history people must be willing to accept the imperfections of their ancestors and often their own imperfections. People must also be willing to accept changes that may fundamentally alter their way of life. This will be difficult for any person. However, many individuals and societies have been and will continue to face these choices. The telephone switchboard operator who lost her or his job when the switchboard was eliminated was probably not ready to find a new career and change their life but the change in technology left them with no choice. The sooner that this person recognized that technology was going to replace his or her job, then the more prepared and enable to adjust to the change would the person be when it happened.

To be receptive to the lessons of history people must maintain an open mind. They must be receptive to new ideas. To be receptive to new ideas people must be aware and think about ideas and concepts not just rules and facts. As the saying go "Practice makes perfect". If a person is only concerned with rules and facts and never thinks about the concepts and ideas, then the person will be less likely to accept new ideas. They are comfortable with their rules and facts. They don't want to be bothered with new ideas. The lessons of history are not about rules and facts. They are about understanding the important ideas and concepts and recognizing when and how to apply to them to the present and future. History teaches rules but extracts a heavy price when those rules are applied but the circumstances have changed. Many societies have been decimated because their military policies were based on fighting the last war. The French Army was unprepared to fight the Nazi army because their whole strategy was base on fighting the same way as they had in the First World War. The rules that they were following were not applicable to a war that was fought with tanks and planes. They were not receptive to the lessons of history. In this case the lesson that new technology can change how battles and wars are fought and won.

To be truly successful people must be more than receptive to new ideas, they need to look for change and seek it out. If a person waits for others to identify the change and to bring it to them, then they will have to be content to be the followers and not the leaders. The leaders are those individuals who are able to identify the change and react to it before others have recognized it.

What type of person are you?

────────────◆────────────

"Why" is an important question that is not asked frequently enough. Too many times people accept or ask only what they need to know to get something done not why the rules work. Children have inquiring minds. They are always asking "why". Most parents get tired of trying to answer all of the why questions that their toddlers ask them. Their parents and society often stifle the inquisitive nature that children exhibit as toddlers as the child grows older.

A child does not lose the need to understand "why". They are taught not to ask "why". This is accomplished in many ways but the net effect is that they become willing to accept cookbooks instead of demanding to know why they are doing something and why what they are doing works. The effect on people is different. Some people retain a more conscious need for this understanding than others. Others become very comfortable with rules and procedures and don't need the understanding.

People are born with this innate need to know why (to understand). As with all innate instincts it is stronger or more dominant in some people than it is in others. The ability to communicate information as a set of rules is an ability that is unique to humans. It is unique to humans because complex rules can't be communicated to new individuals without oral or written languages. It is especially dependent on written language because most people are not able to remember a long set of rules if they are only told them. They need to write them down. When a mother bird is teaching her offspring to fly, she doesn't have the ability to explain in detail what they must do. She relies on showing them the general concepts and the offspring's basic instincts.

The evolution of language has allowed mankind to communicate very specific and detailed directions. Without oral and written languages we would be forced to communicate information in very general terms. Within the animal kingdom some animals have learned to communicate very specific information but only when it relates to a specific activity or situation. Bees are able to communicate the exact location and nature of a source of nectar by a dance. There are other examples of specific communication capabilities among other animals. However, they are always limited to describing specific activities or things that are very important to that species. Language has given humans the ability to shape our environment, accumulate and pass down ever increasing amounts of information from one generation to the next, and to do many other wonderful things. These are the benefits of language.

The negative side of language is that it has permitted and in some ways forced us to develop rules and to ignore the needs for understanding. A person can buy a cookbook and follow the recipes and create a great meal. A person does not have to spend the time to learn why the recipe generating a great meal. With the explosion of information that is occurring today, society must rely on learning specific information in some situations. People can not be expected to acquire a deep understanding of all subjects that affect them. However, society needs to have a very strong understanding of what is gained and what is lost when only rules are communicated or learned. Different styles of communication have different risks and rewards. Intelligent decisions must be made based on understanding all of these factors. A person's ability to evaluate these factors and to make an intelligent decision will be affected by the person's preferences and experiences.

People are born with a need to understand. As with all human characteristics this need is stronger in some individuals than it is in others. Some people are more athletically inclined than others. This is true with all traits. Any person can increase his or her athletic skills through training and practice. However, a man who is only 5 foot tall is unlikely to ever become a champion shot-putter no matter how much time and effort he devotes to it. The advantage that others are given because of their size is too great. It would be more prudent to channel his energy into other endeavors. There will always be times when people must accept conditions as they are. Everyone has only a limited amount of time on this earth so it is not possible to know everything or do everything.

Some people are procedural or detail oriented and others are idea oriented. The world needs both types of people. Also, different situations may dictate what type of behavior is appropriate. When assembling a child's toy, it is best not to question why but to simply follow the directions. The time and effort required to understand the reasons for doing something may not be justified. For someone who needs to understand why, this may cause that person stress and tension because he or she is not allowed to understand why. The directions merely instruct the person to perform each step in order. They do not provide any insight into why the particular order of steps is important. A person who does not accept directions without understanding may have a difficult time with this situation. They may have to assemble a lot of things only to have to disassemble them because they didn't follow the instructions carefully enough and didn't understand why it was important to do certain steps in order. One reason that a person repeats this behavior is that this process does allow them to gain an understanding. This is a reward for a person that needs to understand why.

Because different situations require people to respond in different ways, it is important that people understand what type of person they are. By understanding their natural tendencies they will be better able to cope with situations that fall outside of their comfort zone. For a shy person their comfort zone for interacting with other people is to deal only with people that they know. A self-conscious person is in their comfortable zone when they are one of a group not an individual. Everyone has a comfort zone for different aspects of their personality. People learn to deal with these traits. There are tests to identify whether an individual is an introvert or an extrovert, thinking or feeling, etc. Courses like the Dale Carnegie Public Speaking course increase an individual's comfort zone and equip them to better deal with situations outside of their comfort zone. How people learn and how they deal with ideas and rules is also a personality trait. An individual must understand their comfort zone before they can work to increase it. Therefore, people need to understand how they respond to rules and concepts if they are to expand their comfort zone for this trait. Also, an individual is better able to deal with situations that place them outside of their comfort zone if they understand their comfort zone. They may develop and utilize different techniques to deal with these types of situations.

Everyone should be aware of his or her natural tendencies. This understanding will allow them to better deal with new situations. Without this understanding people are bound to their comfort zone and can never grow as individuals. As with any trait an individual can't expect to spend their whole life in their comfort zones. There will always be occasions when an individual needs to operation outside of their comfort zones. If a person is shy, there will be occasions when he or she will need to meet new people or socialize in a group setting. Also, it is when people leave our comfort zones that they learn and grow as individuals. Since there are always situations where either following rules or demanding an explanation would be an inappropriate course of action, people must learn to deal with both types of learning. When there is a danger of physical harm, there is no time to explain. Immediate action is required. This is an example of where it would not be prudent to wait for an explanation. However, there are many other situations where an explanation should be demanded.

Another chapter of the book will discuss what happens when important ideas are turned into a set of rules. Ideas have a power that can be lost when they are institutionalized into rules. The power of ideas is that they can either be applied directly to new situations or they can provide insight on how to handle the new situation. Rules have a different type of power. The power of rules is that they are easy to communication and can easily and quickly be disseminated throughout a large group.

Every human endeavor of any magnitude requires individuals who possess both types of thinking processes. Both types can be very successful in achieving their results. They may each achieve excellent results but the techniques that they use may be very different. The automotive mechanic that operates on a conceptual level may diagnose the problem with a car by listening to the noise of the engine or by driving it. A mechanic that is comfortable with rules and procedures might use a step-by-step diagnostic approach to solve the problem. A step-by-step approach may involve some of the following steps:

1. Check manufacturer's technical notices for known problems.
2. Run engine through diagnostic program.
3. Review diagnostics.

Both methods can be successful in the appropriate situation. A mechanic who does not know the step-by-step procedure for analyzing a problem may not be able to fix a problem that does not fit with his concepts. For instance, if the manufacturer has started using a new technology, then this mechanic will not be able to fix the car until he has been trained in the new technology (understand the concepts that are embodied in the new technology). However, the mechanic who is able to follow the instructions may be able to fix the problem even if he does not understand the new technology. This mechanic will simply follow his normal process, which will lead him to the appropriate solution. However, the mechanic who is able to bypass the step-by-step procedure may be able to resolve many problems more quickly and efficiently.

Individuals alternate between these two types of behavior. They are pulled in both directions. A part of each of them wants to understand the why; the idea, while the other part of them only wants to know how (the directions). As with all human traits the strength of each varies between people. Some people have a strong need to know why, while other people simply want to learn how. Others may exhibit both characteristics depending on the situation. Both types of individuals have their strengths and weaknesses in problem solving situations. In order to be effective in all situations individuals must be able to adjust their behavior to the situation.

It is very important to stress that one type of behavior is not superior to the other. Just as other types of behavior such as being introverted or extroverted are neither good nor bad, being conceptual or procedural (rule oriented) is neither good nor bad. What is true is that the two types of people will perform differently depending on what qualities are important to that situation.

An individual will be most successful when he is able to identify when each approach is appropriate and modify his behavior to conform to the situation. For example, listed below are some conditions that would generally indicate that one should follow directions:

1. Priority to achieve quick results (emergency, deadline approaching, etc.)
2. Low probability of encountering similar situation in the future.
3. Detailed directions available.
4. Need for consistent results.

When any of these conditions are present, then the most productive course of action may consist of teaching and learning the rules to be followed. Many situations will demonstrate all of these conditions such as starting a new job or a temporary assignment. The person who is starting the new job or assignment will need to make a good impression on their management. The first impressions that an individual makes on others are the most important. Following procedures and directions will allow the individual to demonstrate his productivity and establish a favorable impression. Taking time to understand the concepts may adversely effect the completion of the assignment. Therefore, learning the rules is the best course for the individual who has to perform the task.

What is the most effective way for the individual who is instructing the person to perform a task in the type of situation discussed in the previous paragraph? Would this person be better off to try to teach the new hire why they are doing their job or would they be better off just to tell them how to do it. Since in most instances it would require more time to teach them why than to give a set of detailed instructions, it is more productive to teach or give the person who will perform the task a set of instructions. Both participants gain by minimizing the amount and duration of the communication.

Conditions that may indicate that an individual should understand the concepts are:

1. Consequences of inappropriate actions are critical.
2. High probability that similar situations, not the exact situation, will be repeated in the future. A person is more likely to remember directions if they understand why. Their responses to a similar situation will be better if they have a more thorough understanding.
3. The directions are general in nature and must be adapted to each situation.

When any of these conditions are present, then the most effective communication may be instruction in the concepts not just directions. If the consequences of inappropriate actions are critical, then the individual who will perform the task needs to understand why something is being done not just how to do it. Only an understanding of why will allow the individual to understand the consequences of their actions.

If there is a high probability of similar situations in the future, then only an understanding of the concepts can be applied to the new situations. A set of instructions is unlikely to be applicable to the new situation but the concepts can be used to develop a set of instructions or modify the existing ones.

It is unlikely that most situations will conform completely to either of these scenarios. These are just some guidelines to give a feel for when each kind of behavior is appropriate. Judgment must be used in each situation that is encountered. The proper exercise of judgment requires that an individual understand how to apply concepts. Judgment only comes from understanding, not from following directions.

When an individual understands his or her natural tendencies, then they will be able to adjust their behavior based on the situation. A person who is introverted may never become an extrovert but an introverted person can learn to exhibit extrovert characteristics when necessary. People can change and improve themselves only after they have recognized what type of person they are. Awareness always comes before change. Until a person recognizes his or her traits, they can not understand why they react in a certain way.

A discussion of the characteristics of procedural and conceptual individuals will provide criteria that an individual can utilize to evaluate his or her thinking style. The procedure-oriented individual will be discussed first. Then the concept-oriented individual will be discussed next.

When required to solve a problem, the procedure-oriented individual will use a step-by-step method. The method will be based on prior experience or training. This may include researching the problem in a service manual, performing a standard diagnosis routine, etc. In general whenever confronted by a new problem, they will follow the same routine. When they determine a solution, they will apply the solution and be ready for the next problem. They are more concerned with fixing the problem than with the cause of the problem. They need to know the precise steps to be followed. They are concerned with the details and with thorough documentation. When they are shown how to do something, they are content and only need to learn or document the precise steps to be taken.

The procedure-oriented person is satisfied with the facts and rules. Give them a set of procedures to follow and they are off and running. They want to get to the results. Don't waste their time on esoteric issues like why. They want to be taught how to accomplish the task not why they need to do it. They may become irritated when someone tries to explain the process instead of just teaching or demonstrating the steps. They are impatient with learning why. This takes too much time and effort. They want to start using the information. When teaching this type of person, they will attempt to record each specific step in detail so that they can reproduce the exact step in the future.

A concept-oriented person will attack the same problem in a different manner. This individual will be more concerned with the cause of the problem; spending more time trying to relate the current problem to prior problems, analyzing what caused the problem, etc. This kind of person is unlikely to turn to a set of procedures until they have completed their own analysis. After they have completed their own analysis that may require a little or a lot of time, they may employ a methodical process to solve the problem. A concept-oriented person is more concerned with understanding the cause of the problem than with its solution. This type of person may appear to jump to conclusions about the problem or its solution and then seek information to confirm their belief. This person may be more interested in the knowledge than the results.

A concept-oriented person is more concerned with gaining an understanding of the process: Why the process is important, how it works, or why am I doing it. The information that is learned is probably more important to this type of person than the utilization of the information. This type of person may become annoyed or irritated when they are forced into situations where they are only given a set of procedures to follow. This type of person will probably not take a lot of notes when being taught something. They will concentrate on trying to understand the concepts and not write down as much information as the procedure oriented person. They will be more concerned with the general flow than the specific actions.

A procedure-oriented person may feel that the concept person can not follow directions. A concept person may believe that a procedure person is merely an order taker or paper shuffler. When either trait is taken to extreme, this may be the result. Just as the behavior of extremely introverted individual may be incomprehensible to an extremely extroverted individual, the same is true of concept and procedural individuals.

A person's reaction to a learning experience is also indicative of that person's orientation. A concept person will ask, "Why does it work that way?" or "Why do I need to do things a certain way?" The concept person may also ask, "How does it work?" A procedure person would ask, "How do I do it?" or "What are the required steps?" Even if the person does not voice these questions, they will be asking themselves these questions subconsciously. A person who is anxious to learn how to do something so that he or she can begin using this knowledge is procedure oriented. A person who is anxious to learn why is concept oriented.

How you react to a new situation is also an indicator of how you think. When we are placed in new situations, we will tend to revert to our natural tendencies. A person who has learned to overcome his shyness in school may become shyness again when he enters a new environment like the workplace. The learned behavior may have to be re-learned so that it can be applied to the current situation. Therefore, if a person's tendency in a new situation is to look for a procedure to follow, then the person is probably a procedure person. If the person seeks to relate a new situation to an old situation to understand it, then he or she is probably a concept person.

If the person is conceptual oriented, the process of arriving at this concept was probably a conscious effort. A concept person may annoy their boss or co-worker because they ask a lot of questions about what they are doing and not about how to do it. A concept person will keep asking questions until he/she has developed a conceptual understanding of the process or job. There is no assurance that the boss or co-worker will readily share this knowledge with them. Since the knowledge of the reason, concept, or idea bestows power on its owner and the boss or co-worker might not want to share this type of knowledge. In addition they may not possess it. It is also possible that the boss or co-worker may have an incorrect concept as they may have only been taught how to do the job not why. If the concept person does not acquire the knowledge from his boss or co-workers, then she (he) will consciously evaluate the directions receive along with any other information available to develop a concept. In any case the final understanding or concept may or may not be consistent with real concept.

A procedural person is inclined to keep gathering additional rules and directions as new situations present themselves. No conscious effort will be made to categorize or understand the directions. They will continue to seek directions when a new situation arises. However, just because they don't put any conscious effort into it, does not mean that their minds will not subconsciously develop its own theory or concept. They may not discuss this understanding with anyone else but it will exist. The mind needs to organize everything so it will categorize the available data and develop a neat package (concept). The directions will become consistent based on the concept that the person has subconsciously formulated. Again, the final understanding or concept may or may not be consistent with reality.

Our background also has a lot to do with how we think. We are born with a need to understand. Most parents would be very rich if they had a dime for every time their small child had asked them "why". However, after a lot of effort most parents with help from society in general are able to suppress this habit in most children. The problem is that people need to understand when it is appropriate to ask questions and when it is appropriate to follow directions. It is this ability that will make them successful. Someone who follows directions blindly or who spends all of his time trying to understand ideas will not be very successful in this world.

There are many factors that affect a person's personality in this case their thought process. They are born with natural tendencies. They learn behavior from their parents, siblings, and friends. What they learn from others can either reinforce their natural tendencies or cause them to stretch their comfort zones. Their experiences in school and at work will also influence them. All of these things interact to shape a person's personality. A person should understand his or her natural tendencies so that he or she can respond to these influences. Also, society needs to understand how business and educational methods are reinforcing or stretching the natural tendencies of the individual that comprise society. If the most successful individuals are those who can master both type of behavior and use them both effectively, then society's goal should be to move all people to this balance. The ways that people deal with individuals in business or school would ideally help everyone to expand their comfort zone and move them to the middle.

Everyone is born with a need to understand "why". The strength of this need varies from person to person. People also have a need to achieve tangible results. Everyone likes to be able to step back and say that "I built that" or "I accomplished that". These two needs are in conflict in as much as the need to understand may lengthen the time required to accomplish a goal. Delaying the completion of the goal postpones the realization of the satisfaction of accomplishment. The relative strength of these two drives helps to determine whether the person is concept or procedure oriented. A concept person has a very strong need to understand why and may not be concerned with results. A procedure person has a very strong need to accomplish their goals and may not be concerned with understanding why.

The United States has always benefited from the diversity of its people and cultural as it has been a melting pot for the people of the world.

The story of the growth and rise of the United States to a superpower has shown when:

1. All types of individuals are allowed to flourish and grow
2. The skills of each individual are utilized to the maximum
3. Each individual is allowed to expand his or her skills

that society benefits from the utilization of all of the talents of the individuals that may up the society. A society that limits the opportunities of its members or discourages the growth of its members is not utilizing all of its resources.

There is a tendency in the United States for many individuals, organizations, etc. to reinforce the desire to achieve through learning how to do things and to minimize the importance of understanding why. The parents of many children become frustrated with answering "why" and attempt to stop this type of question. For many or most individuals their first work experience will be as teenager in a job where they are required to follow detailed instructions with no explanation of why. Results that are quickly and consistently achieved with little wasted time or resources are important. MacDonald has been very successful by delivering hamburgers to their customers that have a consistent quality for a reasonable price. This would not be possible if each new employee needed to learn why the MacDonald process of making a hamburger works efficiently. However, in order to progress society needs citizens that can reason, who can apply what they have learned to new situations, etc not just citizens that follow directions.

If everyone in a society were conceptually oriented, then reinforcing procedural behavior would be beneficial, as it would be pushing people in general to the middle. It is the belief of the author of this book that this is not true. The distribution of most traits in a society conforms to a normal distribution with a bell shaped distribution curve. There are always some extremes. If the trait is height, then there are midget and giants but most people are grouped around the middle or median height. The personal observations of the author would tend to indicate that more individuals tend to be procedural than conceptual. If this is true, then it is likely that the majority of people are born favoring neither procedures nor concepts. They are in the middle of the normal curve with the median on the procedural side. Since the environmental factors that influence their development reinforce their procedural side, they end up on the procedural end of the curve as adults.

People are born with concepts and ideas ingrained in their subconscious minds. A beaver doesn't have a detailed plan to follow when he builds a dam but he has a good concept. The beaver must improvise with the materials that he has available. A beaver is born with the concepts that are required to build a dam. The beaver adds to this base as he observes other beavers and he tries to build a dam himself.

Concepts and ideas provide a foundation for learning. Concepts are what integrate the mountain of facts that people are exposed to into knowledge. Knowledge of facts can not be applied to new situations, knowledge of the concepts that support the facts are needed. The human brain differs from a computer in that computers are very good with precise information but they are only now beginning to be programmed with fuzzy logic, which would be more akin to a concept. The human brain is more able to deal with concepts than with mountains of data.

Even though, the human brain is geared to deal with concepts not procedures, there are several reasons why people are still drawn to procedures. The first is that procedures allow us to quickly become proficient in new or difficult tasks. An individual doesn't need to expend the time and effort to understand why or how something works when they are required to do a new task. This provides the individual with instant gratification. The person has accomplished something. Modern mass production techniques require that difficult tasks be broken down into a series of simple tasks that can be quickly learned and perfected. Procedures also ensure consistency and reduce variation. However, the most effective employee is usually the one who understands both the procedures to be followed to ensure consistency and the concepts and ideas behind the procedures.

Another reason that people are drawn to procedures is that procedures are easier to learn than concepts. The development of language especially written language has allowed humans to record, store, and communicate tremendous amounts of detailed information. It is easier to write up procedures to communicate how to do a certain task than it is to explain why the task needs to be done, why it is important to do them in a certain sequence, etc. Therefore, people usually take the path of least resistance and document procedures and rules not ideas and concepts. For a person who is more procedure oriented, this orientation will be reinforced because he will automatically reverted to the behavior that is natural when he is placed in a new or stressful situation.

The third reason is that following procedures and rules becomes a habit. After being constantly forced to learn procedures, it is become a path of least resistance. As societies become more complex and there are more people to instruct, there is less time and resources to expend on teaching concepts. The increase in complexity of modern life leads institutions to teach more procedures than concepts.

In summary, people are motivated by both concepts and procedures. The strength of these conflicting drives is determined by several factors: personal preferences, education, and environment. The ability to succeed is dependent on using both types of approaches when they are appropriate. There are a number of factors that tend to push people into becoming more and more process oriented. If these factors succeeded in moving the bulk of society to be in the middle neither procedural nor conceptual, then this would be beneficial for society. If bulk of society starts out positioned on the conceptual side of the continuum, then these pressures have the possibility of pushing society toward the middle. If the majority of society starts out with no predisposition for one or the other or has a preference for procedures to start with, then it is not good for the majority of our societal reinforcements to be in the direction of procedures.

It is important that individuals understand whether their thought processes are conceptual or procedural. This will help to them to deal with the situations that place them outside of the comfort zones. When people learn what their weaknesses are, they can begin to work on these weaknesses. These weaknesses may not become strengths but recognition and effort can help individuals reduce the negative aspects of these weaknesses.

Concepts Vs. Procedures

———————◆———————

Having a good idea does not ensure success. The idea must be implemented. Ray Kroc saw a good idea that the MacDonald's brothers had developed and turned it into a corporate giant. People need the ability to recognize concepts and then develop and implement the rules that encapsulate those concepts. Choosing the appropriate type of behavior based on the circumstances is a valuable expertise. Both types of behavior have advantages and disadvantages. Therefore, this chapter will be devoted to considering some of the differences and advantages of both concepts and procedures.

The two types of behaviors that people exhibit, how the strengths of these behaviors differ in individuals, and why these behaviors are stronger or weaker in different individuals have been discussed. The advantages and disadvantages of each type of behavior will not be discussed. The reader might now ask 'Why does it matter if people think in terms of ideas or procedures?' People may have different thinking patterns but their underlying concepts or understandings drive them all. Everyone has tasks or assignments that they must accomplish. Does it matter how they accomplish them?

There are several things that would have to be true if it did not matter how things were accomplished. The first is that following a set of rules would always have to produce the same results. The second is that the costs to teach and learn procedures would have to be the same as the cost to teach and learn concepts. Finally, individuals with differing levels of knowledge about the concepts and procedures would have to arrive at the same results with the same amount of effort. These rules are not true. First, rules do not always produce the same results if the superficial facts of the situation are the same but there are additional conditions that are different. These additional conditions may profoundly change the situation but the rules do not comprehend these facts so they are ignored. Second, the costs to develop and articulate the concepts will almost always be different than the costs to develop or articulate procedures. Thirdly, individuals have different abilities to learn and communicate concepts. Therefore, there are differences between the knowledge of concepts and the knowledge of procedures. This chapter will discuss these differences.

First, concepts will be considered. A concept is like the light bulb that is displayed above the head of a comic strip character when she (he) has a good idea. **Concepts drive the endeavors of everyone.** Concepts allow people to apply their knowledge to new and different situations. For example, personal computer software developers have been successful adapting a concept (point and click) to their products so that users feel comfortable experimenting with new programs.

Concepts are power. Anyone who has started a new job should be able to relate to the situation where they start a new job and are given a set of directions to follow but are not told why they are to follow them. Because they only have a set of directions, they must ask their boss or co-worker whenever they encounter a situation not covered by their directions. This provides the boss or co-worker with substantial power over them. The person with the knowledge to handle the new situation is in a power position and therefore, more valuable to the organization. The power is derived from the knowledge not from the person's position in the organization. The person with the knowledge may be at the same or lower level in the organization but still have substantially more power in the other.

Concepts are very adaptable. A concept can cover a multitude of situations. It will not embody specific actions for any situation but it will allow its possessor to analyze the situation and develop the appropriate actions. When a person teaches someone else the underlying concepts, they are transferring the real knowledge and power that they possess. The ability to adapt to new situations is very valuable since the world is always changing. Rules that work today are likely to be obsolete soon.

Concepts are like opinions. Everyone has one. However, unlike opinions, people may have a difficult time communicating them. It is more difficult to communicate an idea than it is to communicate specific rules to follow. Sometimes, it is difficult to communicate them because the ideas don't exist in the conscious portion of people's brains if the person has never consciously developed the idea. Subconsciously, people act on the idea but they have never undertaken the effort to make the idea part of their conscious thoughts. This can occur when people have worked in a specific area for a long time and have developed a thorough knowledge of the area but have never communicated this knowledge to anyone else. The act of bringing the concept into the conscious portion of their mind requires that they construct the idea in a way that it can be communicated. If an idea cannot be communicated, then it is not understood on a conscious level. Though, the subconscious mind may still understand it.

Most of the activities that people perform each day are not accomplished by following a rigid set of procedures; they are accomplished by understanding general concepts. If a person meets someone that they haven't seen for a long time, they don't execute a set of rules to determine if he or she is the same person. The mind has a general concept or understanding of how people change over time and the mind subconsciously applies this concept to compare the person's present appearance with their previous appearance. The mind does this very efficiently and quickly without applying any conscious rules or procedures.

Another example would be the differences in cars. One car may have bucket seats and a gear shift lever on the console; the next may have a gear shift lever on the column. The gages and dials are different but most people still feel comfortable with driving either type of car without any procedures because these differences still fall within our concept of a car and how to operate it. However, if a person were asked to drive an experimental car that didn't have a steering wheel or gearshift, they may feel uncomfortable and need some instructions on how to operate the car. The mechanics of operating the car would not fall within their concept of how a car should be operated. Most of tasks that a person performs daily are accomplished with little conscious thought. Many of these tasks are very complex and would be difficult or impossible to develop a set of procedures to handle them but people perform them with little effort or thought.

Concepts are a major factor in how people learn. Information that does not fit a person's conceptual model is not processed by the mind or it is not stored in long-term memory. The human brain is programmed to only recognize and remember information that fits into the conceptual view of a situation that is being studied. Concepts are visors that filter the information that the mind must deal with. Concepts filter the information that the mind processes. The mind must determine what information is relevant and what information is irrelevant only the information that is relevant will be processed by the mind. The eyes and the ears transmit visual and audio information to the brain but the brain does not always process this information. The brain chooses what information is relevant and reacts or stores only that information.

When a company's employees have an erroneous understanding of their assignments, then problems can arise even if the employees are following the directions that they have been taught. An erroneous understanding will cause them to ignore or miss a subtle change in a situation that could have a profound effect on their actions. The importance of this change will be missed. People's minds only process information that it believes is relevant and ignores the rest. The mind uses concepts and ideas as filters. Only information that matches with their understanding or beliefs is accepted and processed. Information that does not fit with our beliefs is not accepted. It is important to be able to filter out extraneous information as humans in modern society are overloaded with data. Therefore, people need to be aware of their beliefs if they are to have any chance of recognizing changes that may necessitate modifications to their beliefs.

Concepts are the "why": Why am I doing this, what happens when I do this, why does it work, etc. Think conceptual and act procedural. People need to be aware of their conscious perception of the concepts because their perceptions will guide their thoughts and actions. Concepts determine how a situation is viewed. One of the buzzwords in business today is *paradigm shift*. People are warned that they must be aware of changing paradigms; paradigm shifts. Why do people have a hard time in recognizing a paradigm shift? People do not recognize paradigm shifts because they are blind to the changes that are occurring. When they don't think consciously about the concepts that drive their actions, then they will not be able to see the important changes that should alter their actions. When people only follow procedures and don't analyze concepts, their minds will only see those facts that have assigned an importance. An understanding of the concepts will determine what information has been ranked as important and how important it is. New data will be ignored and disregarded. Therefore, people need to think conceptually. This opens the mind up to new possibilities.

In summary, concepts have the following qualities:

1. They are adaptable to new situations.
2. They can exist in our conscious thoughts or our subconscious thoughts.
3. They are difficult to communicate.
4. They provide the foundation for most of our routine daily activities.

5. They act as filters to our acquisition of new knowledge.

6. They are embodied in "why" questions.

A person who is not conceptually oriented may not be consciously aware of the concepts that drive his or her actions. Ideas might not be a part of the person's conscious thought process but the concepts still exist in the subconscious mind. To utilize the power of a concept does not require that a person be able to communicate the concept. The power comes from the insight that our conceptual understanding gives us in new situations. Our minds will employ this power either consciously or subconsciously. Therefore, either type of person utilizes their ideas. Though, they arrive at their ideas from different directions. A procedural person may have a very good understanding of the underlying concepts but is not able to articulate this understanding to other people or even realize that they have it. The understanding is always a subconscious level.

There is a fundamental difference between a conscious and subconscious concept. A conscious concept can be evaluated against new circumstance to determine if it is still applicable. This evaluation may determine that the concept is not applicable even though the circumstances are very similar. Likewise, the concept may still be applicable even though the circumstances seem to be very different. If the concept is only known at a subconscious level, then these conscious processes of evaluating the concept against circumstances that don't seem to fit the original situation will not be perform. Since the concept is only known at a subconscious level, the subconscious mind will only apply the concept where the circumstances match the requirements as established in the subconscious mind.

Procedural people don't spend a lot of time thinking about the concepts that direct their actions. This makes it more difficult for them to communicate their ideas. Their ideas might not be a part of their conscious thought process but they still exist in their subconscious mind. To utilize the power of a concept in situations which are consistent with it does not require that the person be able to communicate that concept. Therefore, either type of person can utilize their ideas. Though, they arrive at their concepts from different directions. Also, the procedural person can only apply the concept to a situation that fits into their original set of requirements. A conceptual person can consciously analyze a new situation to determine if a concept can be applied to the new situation even if the facts of the situation are different.

Procedures are the embodiment of "how": How is something done, what are the steps, etc. Procedures allow for the duplication of results. If a rigid set of steps is performed, then a certain outcome is expected. In the competitive environment of modern society, it is important to be able to give people a set of steps to follow which will produce a predictable result. In an industry like fast food chains with high employee turnover it is necessary to make people productive quickly and to produce consistent results. This type of situation is perfect for procedures and rules. It is unrealistic to expect that McDonald's or Burger King would take the time and effort to explain the fast food business or even the preparation of fries to a new employee who will probably only work for a few months. The business requires that the employees become productive almost immediately.

Armies have historically operated on a procedural basis. Soldiers were given orders and they were expected to carry them out. Only the senior leaders were aware of the overall strategy. There were two reasons for this. The first is the factor of speed. It takes less time to disseminate orders this way. Speed of communication and action is always important in a battle. The second factor is secrecy. If a soldier was captured, then he has very little knowledge to given to the enemy. The overall strategy is what is important not the individual actions. The practice of giving each individual only the information that he needs is prevalent in many organizations not just the military. Procedures allow us to limit the amount of information that is transferred to other people so that they can perform their job.

Procedures facilitate the division of large tasks into smaller pieces. A large task can be broken into smaller pieces that can then be given to different people to perform. There is no need for each person to understand how his or her piece fits into the puzzle to complete the larger task. They just have to follow the steps in their procedure. Without the division of labor inherent in mass production modern society could not have the standard of living that it does.

So, why does society need to "act procedurally" if people should be thinking conceptually? In order to be effective people need to follow the rules or at least they need to be able to explain why and how they are modifying the rules. Understanding the concepts gives them the knowledge to know when and how to modify our rules. When changes are needed, this information must be communicated to the other individuals that are affected by these changes.

Just because someone possesses the correct concept to guide his actions, does not mean that he will achieve good results. A person may know what needs to be done. However, this is of little value unless the person can implement it correctly and in a timely manner. Procedures provide people with a methodology for insuring consistent results. A trip to any McDonald's restaurant demonstrates how procedures can generate consistent results. The more detailed and specific the instructions are the more consistent the results assuming there has been no change in the underlying facts.

In today's environment where every business is subject to intense competition, it is very important to continually improve the goods and services that society produces. As businesses increase their efficiency, they reach a point where any gains in efficiency are very small and they must look for drastic changes to gain more efficiency. In order to make drastic changes companies must understand the concepts that drive their business. There are two ways that a company can improve its efficiency. The first way is to improve their procedures to reduce the amount of variation in their process. This requires attention to the procedures and processes. The second way is to completely redesign or re-engineer the processes, the product, or the service. In order to redesign a process, product, or service the underlying concept that drives the process must be thoroughly understand.

When people view a picture that can be viewed as two pictures, their subconscious mind fills in the missing information. A person's mind is able to extrapolate the missing data that is not shown so that it matches the mental concept of what should be there. The person's eyes don't see the picture but the mind fills in the missing information. Conversely, the mind may ignore additional information that does not fit the picture that the mind believe is being seen. If the word *the* is repeated in a sentence, most people would read over it without realizing that it was there. Their eyes would see it but your mind would not process it because the mind knows that there should not be two *the's* in a row. The same is true when the mind receives information that doesn't match the concept that the mind has decided is correct. The information is dropped and not processed.

No one is immune to the tricks that the mind plays on people. It is part of the human heritage. If people had to process every bit of information that they receive from our eyes, ears, nose, etc., they would be less effective and not able to make rapid decisions. Concepts allow people's minds to organize and categorize the information that they receive. By organizing and categorizing the brain is able to make split second decisions based on limited information. Procedures do not allow decisions to be made quickly as the steps in the procedures must be followed

Both procedures and concepts have their place in peoples' lives, jobs, and relationships. As with all things it is important to maintain a balance between them. People must understand themselves in order to maintain this balance. Concepts empower people. Procedures don't. Procedures are inflexible and are not adaptable to new situations. They are only applicable to the situation that they were developed for. This is the weakness of procedures. They are customized for a particular situation. Procedures are easier to develop. They are also easy to communicate. It is easy to tell someone to do something. People use procedures to instruct others in how to accomplish a task. There is a limited amount of knowledge transferred in this type of situation. This makes procedures more authoritative in nature than communications that involve the transfer of concepts.

Both conceptual and procedure people will develop a concept to support the directions that they have been instructed to follow. If they have arrived at the correct concept, then they will move into a power position within the organization. However, if they have arrived at an incorrect concept, then they can imperil their career and the organization if they base any actions on their concepts. If they gain the confidence to take action on their own when faced with a new situation and their concept is incorrect, then the consequences could be catastrophic. If their concepts are wrong, then they will be in trouble when they deviate from their directions or the situation changes.

A new worker in an organization will acquire the knowledge (rules and procedures) to handle different situations. Initially, this will consist of additional directions to be used if a given situation arises. As the person becomes more experienced, he will develop his own concept of why specific tasks are performed. The concept that they develop may be consistent with the real reason or it may not. A person may arrive at this concept through a conscious effect or it may have been arrived at completely subconsciously. However, every person will develop a concept that fits knowledge that is available. If the concept is correct, then the person can use this understanding to move into a power position in the organization. If the concept is wrong, then the person and the whole organization may suffer. Correct concepts provide power but incorrect concepts are very dangerous.

Everyone needs to be able to recognize his or her personal style of thinking. This will allow them to analyze their strengths and weaknesses.

Different situations in life require that people respond in different ways. People need the ability to deal with all types of situations.

Reconciling our Beliefs

◆

The last two chapters have discussed how some people are inclined to think conceptually and others are procedural. How people think also affects a their performance in different situations. In some situations a conceptual person will perform better than a procedural person and it will be reversed in other situations. This chapter will discuss another human characteristic that pressures people into thinking procedurally. Humans have a difficult time reconciling their feelings on moral or ethical issues where these issues involve concepts that they have strong feelings for or against. There are many examples of this. Everyone faces these types of dilemmas.

Two examples from the conservative viewpoint will be discussed. The first involves personal freedom and the right to assisted suicide. An individual may be supportive of the rights of individuals and less government. This type of individual would justify a belief in less taxes and allowing people to decide how much they should be taxed. This would be consistent with the philosophy of personal freedom and less government control. Therefore, an individual can exercise control over his life. This is a noble and worthwhile goal in any society. Everyone wants the maximum control to live their lives as they choose. A belief in the rights of individuals and less government should be consistent with a belief in assisted suicide. However, many individuals who believe in fewer taxes are also against assisted suicide not because it is bad for the person who truly wishes to die but because it is bad for society. This is not consistent with a philosophy of personal freedom and less government control. This creates a dilemma for an individual with these beliefs.

The second example deals with the issue of abortion. Many people are strongly against abortion because they believe that the right of the fetus to live exceeds the right of the woman to control their bodies. However, many of these same people would be opposed to the involuntary removal of organs from a dead body. The issues are basically the same. A person who is dying because one of their organs is failing would like the same rights that the fetus has (the right to command the use of another's body for their survival). This person has no claim on the organs of a corpse. Many individuals die every year waiting for organ donations. However, the donation of an organ is completely voluntary. Many people don't consider that the rights of the individual to live could be equal to the rights of the deceased to be buried with all of its organs. If the right to live is to override a woman's ability to control her own body, then at least the rights of a dying person in need of an organ transplant should be considered when evaluating how the need for organ donations is satisfied.

The donation of blood that causes little pain or inconvenience is completely voluntary because people have the right to control their bodies even at the expense of other people's lives. Most people support the concept that the donation of any organ or a person's blood should be voluntary. Many people die every year while waiting for an organ donation when their lives could be saved if more people would donate their organs when they die. However, there is no passion from those people who are anti-abortion to force the donation of organs from the deceased. If the rights of the unborn fetish exceed the rights of the woman, then why does the rights of the dead exceed the rights of the terminally ill. Most individuals do not see any contradiction in these two positions. Is this because the positions are not contradictory or is it because people are able to keep the underlying concept in their subconscious mind so that they do not have to deal with the contradiction?

The issue of welfare will demonstrate the problem of reconciling our belief from a liberal standpoint. Many studies have shown that welfare does not raise the standard of living for its recipients. It tends to create an environment where the cycle of poverty is perpetuated from generation to generation. A person who is pro-welfare can be blind to this fact. The depth of the problems that welfare causes may be argued but the fact that is causes some problems can not be argued. The concept of welfare is to ease pain and suffering not to cause problems. For many individuals the long-term effort of welfare is to create a dependency on it. It is difficult for many individuals to recognize this contradiction. Until this contradiction is recognized, there is no possibly of finding solutions to this problem.

In these types of situations it is difficult to reconcile the belief in a general concept with the differing positions. One way that this conflict can be resolve is to deny the existence of the conflict. The human mind has many ways to deal with contradiction and one is denial. The effectiveness of this technique is enhanced if the mind is able to separate conscious positions from any connections to the subconscious concepts that are driving these positions. The conscious mind is very good at masking human's true motivation when those humans do not want to recognize those motives. How many individuals are ready to honestly confront the motives for many of their acts? People will profess one reason for doing something because they are unable to admit the real reason.

This psychological defense mechanism helps humans to maintain their mental stability by eliminating the stress of psychological conflict. It also is a reason to not consciously analyze and formulate the concepts that drive a person's actions. Each time that this defense mechanism is used the easy and more routine it becomes to ignore all concepts and to concentrate on the rules and procedures. This will reinforce any tendency that an individual may have for procedures and provide a disincentive for a conceptual individual.

The ability to recognize these types of conflicts does not mean that the individual will be able to resolve them but this recognition may allow him or her to cope them with better. Also, this recognition will help people to understand and to be more tolerant of the views of others. When people accept their own conflicts and others raise those conflicts, then they will be less likely to become angry and agitated. This is very beneficial to society. People do not have to support or accept the beliefs of others but they need to tolerant of the others' beliefs.

If people would learn to examine and accept the reasons for their beliefs, then they should be better able to discuss those beliefs with others and understand why others have different beliefs. This will require that people accept some amount of psychological tension when their beliefs are contradictory.

Learning and Thinking Style

———————— ◆ ————————

How does a person's learning style or type of thinking effect that person? It certainly effects the type of work that the person enjoys, how he or she will respond to different learning environments, how he or she will deal with others, and others behavior.

A person's learning style could affect the type of work that they will enjoy. Since work consumes such a large portion of a person's adult life, it is important that they understand how their learning and thinking style will affect their work life. The most obvious observation is that the ability to switch between both styles and to be effective when using either will be the most benefit to a person in his or her career. If a person can only do what they are told to do or they can't get the details correct, then they are not going to be very valuable to an employer. The inability to effectively utilize both types of behavior is a definite weakness. Since most people want more money, responsibility, etc.; individuals should work on those things that they are not good at and try to take the maximum advantage of their strengths. Before this can be done, the person must recognize what their strengths and weaknesses are.

A conceptually oriented individual has one advantage in evaluating their strengths and weaknesses in that they are constantly evaluating the underlying reasons for the things that occur around them. They may also be more comfortable with facing the conflicts between some of their beliefs, actions, etc. If they are, then this will allow them to more objectively evaluate their strengths and weaknesses. A procedural people may be less inclined to evaluate the underlying reason or to face any conflicts in their beliefs, actions, etc.

An individual's style of thinking will also effect how much enjoyment that the individual gain from his or her job. One of the worst side effects of being a conceptually oriented person is that they tend to become bored with their job quickly. If a person analyzes and learns their job on a conceptual basis, then there is less to learn and less opportunity for learning new challenges in a job. Change and the opportunity to learn new skills and tools is one way that a person's job remains fresh and interesting. When people are no longer challenged intellectually by their job, they become bored with it. A real life situation that might occur and how the two types of individual might view it will serve to demonstrate this. The situation is where a decision has been made to switch from Microsoft Excel to Lotus 1-2-3 for business spreadsheets. For anyone who doesn't have a personal computer at home, these are two business spreadsheet packages that are widely utilized in business and for personal budgeting and other applications. When the two software packages are compared as to how certain tasks are performed, they are very different. However, when the concepts of how spreadsheets works and how they are used to accomplish something, then they become very similar. Therein lies the difference.

In this situation the procedural person will be excited about the possibility of learning some new skills: the new syntax of Lotus commands, the new menus, options, etc. The conceptual person will see it as the opportunity to add an entry on his/her resume but little else. One person will focus on the differences between the packages and the other will focus on the similarities. Both see the same thing but their mind filters the information very differently.

A conceptual person is concerned with the concepts and ideas not the details. After he or she has mastered the concept, they will be less interested in the details. Returning to the example of the spreadsheet software one person will be interested in the overall concept of a spreadsheet and how it operates while the other person will want to try out and learn all of the different options and features that the software allows. For example, one person will be excited about actually learning how to write a formula while the other person is content to know that the software has the ability to handle formulas and that the information on how to do it is available if needed. One person is motivated to learn the specific skill while the other is happy to know the general information.

In today's society the rate of increase in the amount of information is phenomenal. However, the rate of increase in detail information is greater that the rate of increase in conceptual information. The person who is interested in the detail is less likely to become bored in any position than the conceptual person. A procedural person is interested in thinking the specific rules while the conceptual person will only want to learn the overall concepts and little of the specific rules.

A person should be aware of his/her learning style so that the person can make the most out of the each learning situations that they are exposed to. A teacher or mentor may have a different approach than the person receiving the instruction, it is important that a person be able to recognize this difference. Ideally, both the teacher and the student would recognize the difference, then several options could be considered for eliminating the difference. The first option is to do nothing. The student will have to adjust his or her behavior to the teacher. Another option would be to get the instructor to change his approach to teaching. This is unlikely to happen in most situations but the student might try it. The third alternative is to develop questions to ask which fit the style of the teacher but allow the student to develop the information that he or she is looking for. This may be easier if the student is a conceptual person and the teacher is procedural than if the situation is reversed. It is easier to develop specific questions that will test the concepts than it is to develop conceptual questions that will elicit specific rules.

When society educates people, it is very important to understand how they learn and what their natural tendencies are. If education is to be effective, it must both challenge the students to expand their horizons and also let them feel good about themselves. It is very difficult to satisfy both of these at the same time. The learning experience needs to be difficult enough so that people are challenged but easy enough so that they are able to succeed. This becomes even more difficult when the variable of learning styles is added to the mix. The person who is procedural should be challenged to think more about the concepts and ideas. The person who is concept biased should be pushed to follow the rules more precisely.

Most formal educational experiences that people are exposed to are procedural based. This is not an indictment of schools or colleges. The formal and informal training that goes on in the business is even more procedural oriented. Too many times in business people are in a hurry so employees are told what to do and no explanation of why it needs to be done is given. As has been mentioned in previous chapters, knowledge represent power and people are not always willing to give away this power and share everything that they know with the new kid on the block. At least in a formal education environment there is less need to hoard this knowledge to maintain a power position.

Therefore, most teaching and learning tends to have a procedural slant. One reason is that it is easier to teach procedures than it is to teach concepts. It is easier to teach a person that the symbol '20 + 2' is equivalent to the symbol 22 than it is to explain the decimal numbering system and our Arabic representations. If a person only learns the procedure that the symbol '20 + 2' equals the symbol 22, then they will only be able to use this procedure and they will not be able to apply this knowledge to other systems. However, if a person has learned the concepts of numbering systems and representations, then he or she will be able to apply this knowledge to new situations such as the binary system used in computers. It is much easier to write down the rules for addition on a blackboard, to test the students on how well they have memorized them, etc. than it is to try to explain why the rules work the way that they do and to show how other systems of rules can be generated from the same concepts (binary or hexadecimal numbering system, etc.). Then after the concept has been explained, how are the students to be tested to determine if they understand these concepts. Additional difficulties arise because some of the students don't care about the ideas but only want to know what the rules are. Therefore, the path of least resistance is to teach procedures and to ignore the basic concepts.

Children start out with a natural instinct or need to understand why. Little children are always asking why. However, when they get into school, the teacher is under pressure to insure that each child is able to perform a list of tasks by the time the school year is over and the student is also under pressure to master these tasks. Therefore, if it is easier to follow instructions, then this is how the teacher will teach and the students will learn. However, the student that is conceptually biased may experience problems or stress just memorizing rules. This student will have difficulties if he or she is not able to extrapolate the concepts from the rules so that they can learn in their own style.

This over emphasis on teaching procedures creates several problems. The first problem is that it re-enforces any natural tendencies that the person has toward learning rules and procedures and ignoring ideas. The second problem is that it ignores the problems or stress that the conceptual oriented person may have with learning procedures. A balanced learning experience should promote the learning experience of both types of people. It should also motivate individuals to work on their areas of weakness. People should be able to utilize both types of abilities. Therefore, the schools and colleges should be encouraged to work on expanding their capabilities in both procedures and concepts.

Another reason for teaching concepts along with the rules is that as procedures are passed from one person to another, information is lost. People become mere robots following instructions. What separates man from computers is the capability to apply his knowledge to new situations. Only ideas can be applied to new situations. Procedures can not be applied to new situations that don't match the original set of circumstances. It doesn't matter whether the rules are how add 2 and 2 or they are the procedures for approving a loan at a bank. Rules can't be applied to new situations when they are encountered. Therefore, when procedures and rules are all that is taught to the new employee, student, etc., something is lost in the process. As the wealth of a country or company is more and more based on the amount of knowledge that is possessed by the citizens of the country or company, the long-term economic wealth of a country or company is jeopardized when the concepts are not transmitted along with the procedures. The ideas are what are of long-term value, not the rules.

The next reason deals with false concepts and ideas. If the concepts or ideas are not taught, then students, employees, etc. will develop their own concepts to categorize and organize the rules that they learn. The human mind is not computer that does not need to organize and categorize its information. The human mind needs to categorize and organize information to efficiently manage it. The human mind has difficulty remembering or even recognizing information that does not fit its concept of reality. A person can look at a sentence or picture and not see a word or a problem with the picture because it does not relate to their model of what they should be seeing. The human mind like that of all creatures will not recognize that information which it has some reason to recognize. If the human mind was any different, then people would not be able to process all of the information that all of their senses are sending to it. To be able to make quick decisions people's minds have to be able to categorize information as to what is important and what is not important. The mind then only processes the information that it deems to be relevant.

All animals have the ability to recognize sights, sounds, and smells that indicates danger or benefit such as sources of food. This important information must be quickly separated from additional information that the eyes, hears, and nose is providing. In addition, the important information may be less distinctive than the irrelevant information such as a predator that is approaching from the side so it is only see with the peripheral vision. However, the mind is able to ignore the irrelevant that is in abundance and concentrate a small amount of information that may indicate danger.

Rules cause people to categorize only a limited amount of information. Returning to an arithmetic sample, the rule $2 + 2 = 4$ provides little assistance with solving an addition problem in base 2 or 3 numbering system. When a person is faced with new environment where they are asked to add 2 and 2, the person will respond that the answer is 4 even if they have been told that the numbering system is base 3 instead of base 10. Their mind has no reason to recognize the significance of this additional piece of system. It is critical that people's minds be able to limit the amount of information that it processes. However, people need to be aware of concepts and ideas so that they can recognize important information when it is presented to them. People need to periodically bring all of these concepts and idea into their conscious memory to ensure that they are still valid.

People have a tendency to ignore those things that they are familiar with. The more often that rules are confirmed the more people become complacent in analyzing those rules and the concepts that they are built on. This does not cause any problem as long as the circumstances support the concepts. However, problems can arise when the circumstances have changed but the changes are not recognized because people are no longer able to recognize these changes.

Paradigm Shifts

◆

Societies wither and die for a number of reasons. However, the root cause can in many instances be traced back to the fact that the society was unable to respond to a change. The change might have been climatic, a new technology, etc. The Mayan culture of Mexican and Central America thrived for many centuries before the culture was abandoned. One theory for the demise of their culture is a change in the climate. The Mayans were not able to adjust their society to the changed conditions and their society was destroyed. The Mayan people have survived to this day but the social structures that built towering pyramid vanished centuries ago. The Romans conquered a vast empire because their military technology was superior. The Swiss used to dominate the watch industry. They were the first to develop a quartz watch. However, they were enable or unwilling to recognize how the quartz watch would revolutionize the watch industry. The Japanese recognize the potential of the quartz and now the Japanese dominate the watch industry.

The dictionary defines a paradigm as a model or example. A paradigm shift could be described as a change that makes one model obsolete and causes the creation of a new model. The development of computers has caused two paradigm shifts. The first shift occurred with the appearance of commercial mainframe computers. These large computers profoundly altered society. The amount of information that could be gathered and stored rose astronomically. The second shift occurred with the availability of inexpensive powerful personal computers. These two events have fundamentally changed the way people interact, work, learn, etc. The most important change that these events have instigated has been the acceleration of change in society. The amount of knowledge is increasing at an exponential rate and the rate of change in society is also increasing.

A change or a paradigm shift represents both an opportunity and a challenge. When a paradigm shift occurs, then the old model that everyone follows is invalidated and a new model takes its place. When this occurs, the race for economic, social, and political power is restarted. The inherent advantages that the incumbents had possessed may be eliminated in the new structure. Individual positions in the new race are based on their strengths and weaknesses not on their positions in the old model. Therefore, if a person or society was a loser in the race under the old model, then the person or society has a fresh crack at winning the race under the new environment. This is a great opportunity. If you were winning the old race, then your challenge is to react to the new start without any of the advantages that you had previously. Actually, it is usually not a race. Instead of a race, the usual course of events is that one group of people recognizes the paradigm shift before the rest and the race never occurs. The Japanese recognized the potential of the quartz watch and became the dominant watch making society.

Why do some people recognize a paradigm shift before others? Would a society be better able to survive in a constantly changing world if its citizens were more receptive to change? Is the rate of change likely to slow down or increase in the future? How a society answers these questions will help to determine its position in the future world. Likewise, an individual's response to these questions will affect his or her position in the future. Change is inevitable. It is how people or societies respond to these changes that affect the course of their future.

How does thinking conceptual or procedural affect these questions? I believe that an individual who thinks conceptually is more likely to recognize a paradigm shift in its earlier stages. A person who thinks conceptually is more likely to have analyzed the current model to understand the ideas and concepts that allow the model to function and work. An individual who thinks procedurally is more likely to simply follow the rules of the model and not analyze why the model works. Therefore, the first individual is more likely to recognize that the ideas which support the model have changed and that the model needs to be changed that the second individual.

In order to understand how an individual's thought process effects his reaction to a paradigm shift, let's consider three aspects of people's adoption of a paradigm shift. The first is who recognizes the paradigm shift first. The second is how they recognize the change. The third factor is when they recognize and accept that their lives have changed. These three factors will determine how successful a person will be in the future. A person who recognizes the shift early and is able to understand what is causing it will be able to exploit the new environment for his personal benefit. The person or society that misses the window of opportunity may be relegated to a position of follower until the next paradigm shift occurs when they will again have a chance to jump into the lead. The good news for a current follower is that they may have the opportunity to jump into a lead in the near future if a new paradigm occurs. Conversely, the bad news for a leader is that a paradigm shift in the future may leave them in a position of having to strive to catch up with someone who has recognized the shift earlier.

Some people recognize a paradigm shift very early. The people who recognize a paradigm shift are not always those with the most initial advantages. If the paradigm shift is caused by a new invention, it is not always the person or persons who discovered the new invention who recognize the change and benefit from it. The quartz watch is an example of this phenomenon. The Japanese did not invent it but they were the first to profit from it. The individual or group who develops a new technology may or may not recognize how this new technology could be utilized.

People who are experts in the technology, application, industry, etc. which is undergoing change may not be the first to understand the significance of the paradigm shift. Many experts are very skilled in the rules and procedures for using a certain model or theory. However, they may not be as knowledgeable about the ideas that support the model. This type of expert is less likely to recognize the paradigm shift than a person who is familiar with the ideas. The person who is very proficient at applying the model to solve problems may be viewed as more knowledgeable than the person who only understands the ideas that support the model. In spite of this, the person that understands the ideas better is more likely to recognize the paradigm shifts when they occur. A person who only knows rules and procedures will only identify the paradigm until their rules and procedures have stopped functioning. When this happens, the race may be over. The individuals and societies that adjusted to the new paradigm early may have such a lead that the late adapters will have no opportunity to catch up.

The people that are not directly involved with the industry or application may appreciate the opportunity that a paradigm shift creates before those directly involve do. Some people might say that they can't see the forest for the trees. Isn't the forest the idea and the trees are the procedures? Ray Kroc, the founder of McDonald's did not develop the idea for McDonald's. He saw the concept in action and recognized that it had the potential to change the food industry. He was not directly involved in the food industry as he was a salesman of equipment to make milk shakes. However, he recognized the potential of the idea before the McDonald's brothers did.

The second factor is when the people recognize the paradigm shift and adjust to it. The people that recognize the paradigm shift early are in the best position to profit from the shift. In order to capitalize on a paradigm shift there are a number of requirements to be met.

Recognizing the paradigm shift is certainly critical. However, to exploit the knowledge you must still have the capital, desire, etc. to exploit the shift. Therefore, just being one of the first does not guarantee success. The third factor is how people recognize a paradigm shift. This is important because it determines when a person will recognize the paradigm shift and who will be the first to recognize it. The individuals who will first recognize the paradigm shift are those individuals who exhibit two traits. The first trait is that they are always curious about the ideas that support the current model. The second trait is a willingness to accept new ideas. The first trait will lead them to learn and understand why the current model is successful. The knowledge also implies that they will recognize that changes in the concepts will have dramatic effects on the current model. Therefore, they are more likely to be vigilant for changes in the concepts. If you don't know what you should be looking for, then you will never see it.

A person's understanding of the model enhances the third trait (the willingness to accept new ideas). Someone who only knows the rules of the model will be less likely to relinquish the current model than someone who understands the model. The knowledge of the rules provides no assistance in learning and applying the new set of rules. Therefore, this person will be back at the starting line and will have more difficulty in letting go of their current rules. This is a very large step for them. However, for the person who understands the model the change to the new model may not be difficult at all. This person has less to lose with the replacement of the current model.

These traits are those of a person who thinks conceptually. Therefore, a conceptual person is more likely to recognize a paradigm shift earlier than a procedural person. However, many of the skills that are needed to profit from this early knowledge are those that are exhibited by the procedural person. Therefore, people and societies should not be to far from the center of the pendulum.

Know Thyself

———————————— ◆ ————————————

It is easy to hide behind procedures. Everyone has heard or has said to someone "I was only following orders." If people simply follow the orders or directions that they are given, then they don't need to think about what they are doing. They avoid many of the moral dilemmas that they would otherwise have to face. They don't have to deal with their own internal conflicts. As human beings, people have developed many mechanisms for dealing with situations where they are pulled in two directions. These are natural coping mechanisms. Not analyzing and acknowledging the inconsistencies in their beliefs and positions is just one of those mechanisms. Societies need to become more tolerant and open to other's ideas and practices. Moving its citizens away from the procedural end of the continuum can help this. The following section will highlight how this can help.

Not acknowledging the inconsistencies in their beliefs is a very effective technique for individuals. If the conflict is strong enough, then the conscious mind will eliminate all memory of the conflict. When a person is placed into a situation where they have to choose between two opposing values, people will either deny or minimize the significance of the one in order to relieve the stress. What method could be better to deal with these types of internal conflicts than to completely eliminate those conflicts? However, like many other actions that are beneficial to the individual (in some ways) but detrimental to society, this behavior by individuals has grave consequences to society. If they are not able to accept the inconsistencies in their own beliefs, then they can not discuss and resolve the complex issues that confront modern societies. In addition to its consequences to society, it also has a negative side effect on the individual.

What does this have to do with the issue of this book that is the difference in how people think and how these differences effect individuals and societies? However, this coping mechanism in people helps to pressure people into thinking procedurally. This is just one of a number of factors which helps to influence individuals to think. This influence will be detrimental to individuals if they are already prone to thinking procedurally since it is just another factor that will push them more toward that side of the continuum. If the individuals and societies are best served when they stay in the middle of the continuum, then any influence that tends to drive them toward one or the other extreme is harmful. There are other factors that will be discussed in the following chapters that also drive individuals toward the extremes of the continuum. As human society becomes more complex and the population of the world increases, people are more and more confronted with situations where they have to resolve these types of conflicts. Their choices are simple. They can either face their inconsistencies or they can bury them. Unfortunately, it is easier to bury them or deny them than it is to face them.

There are situations where people find it hard to reconcile the conflicting values that they might hold. These situations are difficult and most individuals have strong feelings about them. The issue in this chapter is not to make a decision on the merits of the opposing sides but to consider the conflicts that may arise within an individual. The first social conflict to be discussed is assisted suicide. There are many issues related to assisted suicide but only the issues of personal freedom versus the benefits of society will be discussed.

The right to die is certainly a very important personal right to many people. In certain cultures such as Japan the right to commit suicide is ingrained into the culture and the ritual suicide of the Japanese samurai is a highly structured and was in the past a very honorable method of dying. The Japanese society does not value personal freedom as much as the United States. In the United States suicide is not an honorable way to die. Most states currently or in the past had laws which made suicide illegal. How can societies have different views on personal freedom and suicide? Either, the right to commit suicide has nothing to do personal freedom or there must be some mechanism in operation that allows the individuals in society to reconcile these positions. Since there is certainly an element of personal freedom in the choice of when and how a person dies, there must be something that allows the resolution of the positions. How can a belief in personal freedom be reconciled with a belief that suicide is wrong? The best way for a human is to bury the two concepts in their subconscious and relegate the concepts to a set of rules. Certainly, assisted suicide is different than suicide because with assisted suicide someone beside the victim must actively participate in the suicide. One of the major concerns about assisted suicide is that it may be caused by coercion.

In a sense almost all suicides involve some coercion. Consider the tradition of the Japanese samurai. Does the samurai choose to end his life or is he forced into it? There is nobody standing over him forcing him but he is motivated by the values and traditions of his society. The choice is still left to the individual but the values and traditions of his society leave him little choice. Similarly, in many North American Native cultures the old would leave the tribe to die when they were no longer able to care for themselves. Again, they were following the traditions of their society. In both of these situations the right to die with the approval of society was honorable. Traditions normally develop because they benefit society. In the case of the samurai it was the powerful incentive to be a successful samurai. In the case of the Native

American or any society where much time and energy must be expended just to survive, it is difficult for the society to maintain the older members of society who can no longer support themselves.

In these instances the benefits of personal freedom and the society's welfare are in harmony. What are the benefits to modern societies of discouraging suicides? Modern societies are able to support those individuals in society who are not able to support themselves. This does not mean that societies always want to support them. In the United States there is a very strong tradition of personal freedom. This tradition favors a government that does not interfere in the personal affairs of its citizens. How could a society that values personal freedom so highly want to ban assisted suicide? The partial answer is that there are many disadvantages to society from assisted suicide. Assisted suicide brings with it many unpleasant side effects for society. The first is that it could be abused. Some people may be forced into it because it is the best solution for others and not their free choice. Another is that death is difficult to deal with so people don't like to face it or deal with it. Therefore, the American people views suicide and in particular assisted suicide as harmful to society. However, they still want their personal freedoms.

Therein lie roots of a personal conflict. The American people cherish their personal freedoms but they also understand the negatives of assisted suicide. As with any conflict people try to minimize the conflict between their differing beliefs. They subconsciously use all of their coping mechanisms to resolve the conflict. One of these mechanisms is to reduce the size of their concept of personal freedom. This eliminates the conflict. They eliminate from their concept of personal freedom the right to choose death. The concept of personal freedom has stopped being a concept and has become a set of rules. Personal freedom is the right to do this, this, and this. This is a nice and simple solution for the individual. It eliminates the conflict for the individual.

Another issue that has the possibility of causing a lot of internal conflict is the issue of abortion. Many people oppose abortions on the belief that the unborn child has the right to life. This right to life exceeds or outweighs the woman's right to control her body. This implies that the unborn child has the right to place certain demands on the woman in order that the child can be born. This creates an unavoidable conflict between two concepts: a person's right to life versus the right to control our bodies. To illustrate this conflict, consider how far the right to life should infringe on the right to control one's own body. Does the right to life mean that dangerous behavior such as smoking, drinking, etc. should be illegal for pregnant women? There are no federal or state laws that would require a parent to donate blood or other body parts to their child even if these are required to keep the child alive. The laws of the United States do not give to individuals who are in need of organ transplants the right to take an organ of a deceased person. The individual's right to life is less than the deceased person's right to control his or her body after death. For most individuals there is no conflict between these situations. How can these two scenarios not cause a conflict between the concepts of right to life and personal choice? It does not cause a conflict because the right to life and personal choice are not concepts but a set of rules. This certainly allows the individual to sleep better at night not having to deal with all of these issues.

Having discussed a couple of situations where internal conflicts can arise, let's consider how actions and behaviors of individuals become problems for society. The types of behavior that were discussed above are detrimental to society because they tend to push most individuals away from the middle of the procedural/conceptual continuum and they hinders the resolution of conflicts by society. These behaviors cause three major roadblocks to the resolution of conflicts by society.

The first roadblock is that people become very defensive when their inconsistencies are brought into the lights. Humans try to bury their inconsistencies in their subconscious mind because they don't want to deal with them. Therefore, when someone attempts to force them to deal with these inconsistencies, they go even further into denial. Their basic instincts are to lash out like a trapped animal. Therefore, the commitment to their positions become stronger and it is more difficult for them to compromise. It is then a matter of winning at all cost. It is a personal matter. They must win to prove that they are right and to be able to keep their inconsistencies buried.

The second roadblock is that instead of seeking the best solution for society, people try to win arguments. In any argument, military battle, etc. the first and one of the most important steps in winning is to determine the parameters of the conflict. In a military battle some of the parameters are when the battle will be fought, where the battle will be fought, and how the battle will be fought. The United States lost the Vietnam War because the North Vietnamese were able to force the United States to battle them in a protracted guerilla war. When the United States and its allies defeated Saddam Hussein in Kuwait, the war was fought under terms that were favorable to American technological advantages. The parameters that defined how each war would be fought had a substantial impact on the outcome of each. Determine how, where, and when the battle will be fought and dramatically increase the likelihood of success.

Basketball fan would readily recognize how important it is to establish the tempo of the game. When the two opposing teams have different styles of play (physical vs. finesse or slow and deliberate vs. fast and freewheeling), then how the game is played will usually determine which team will win. For instance, if the referee allows the teams to play physical, then the finesse team will be at a distinct disadvantage and of course the opposite is true if the game is called very closely. The reputation of the teams and the players always has an effect on how the game is officiated and therefore, how the game will be played. The playing field never starts out as level. Coaches and players try to establish the parameters for the game before it is played by complaining publicly about how the other teams plays, complaining to the referees, etc. The goal of these actions is to establish the parameters for the contest.

The reader may ask how does this relate to a conflict in society. To understand how the same type of behavior occurs in society let's consider the issue of abortions. The issue of abortions can cause deep divisions within a society. In the United States it has erupted into violence against doctors and abortion clinics. It has become the only factor that some people consider when voting for elected officials. In short it has become an issue on which few people are willing to compromise or even listen to the views of the other side. It is also an issue in which each side has tried to have the debate over only one aspect of the problem (either the child's right to live or the woman's right to control her own body). If you, the reader are member of a debate team and you want to win the debate, then forcing the other team to fight over your issues is the best strategy to win. This is fine because at the end of the debate both teams shake hands and no one is permanently injured. Though, the loser's pride may be deflated. However, if the issue is a real life problem, then society can not afford win-lose conflicts. The only way that society can arrive at win-win situations is for all parties to recognize the legitimacy of all aspects of the conflict. This is what leads to compromise.

A major roadblock to conflict resolution is respect for the opponent. When people deny the validity of the other person's argument, then the issues can not discussed in an impersonal and logical manner. The conflict becomes a personal matter. By respecting the other person's position and dealing with it in an objective fashion respect is shown for the other person and his or her values. This helps to resolve the conflict and allows compromises to be developed and implemented. However, in order to accept the other person's position people must be willing and able to deal with the internal conflicts that this may cause. If people can not openly and frankly deal with their own beliefs, then there is no way that they can accept the positions of others and they can not respect the other person's position and the argument becomes very personal.

As modern societies become more complex and larger, the need to respect the views and attitudes of others becomes more important. People may not agree with the other person's position but they need to understand it and acknowledge its value. Western societies and in particular the United States have been able to ignore some of these conflicts by expanding into new areas. There have been definite costs to this expand (destruction of native cultures, the degradations of environments, etc.) but it has allowed the United States to minimize the problems caused by intolerance to the beliefs of others within society. This has not included tolerance for others outside of the culture. As the amount of open space shrinks and people are more and more crowded together, it becomes more important that people respect the views of their neighbors. Individual liberties can only survive if they are defended vigorously but used with moderation. When people understand and accept the beliefs and positions of others, they are more likely to show toleration to others and exercise moderation in their own actions. As the world's population grows and the diversity of societies increase, the need for toleration and moderation increases.

All societies demand that the individual relinquish some personal freedom for the good of the society. As the size of the society grows, the amount of freedom that each individual can exercise is reduced. It is preferable that individuals maintain individual restraint so that society does not have to restrict freedoms. However, it is inevitable that society will restrict individual freedoms if they are too badly abused. The reader only has to consider the number of new laws that are passed each year to restrict or regulate behavior within society. Every year more laws are written but few are abolished. It has been said, "Taxes are the price for civilization". It could be said that laws are the price for population growth.

There is only two ways to prevent the loss of freedom of personal choice. The first is toleration and moderation that requires that people understand and respect the views of others. The other is to stabilize and then begin to reduce the population of the world so that when people exercise their personal choices, they are less likely to infringe on the personal freedoms of their neighbors.

There is another feature of modern society that increases the importance of toleration and moderation. This is communication. The era of communications has arrived. There is nowhere on earth where some form of communications is not available that will connect a person to someone else anywhere. There are more sources of information everyday. This means that people are exposed to ideas and beliefs that are opposed to their own on a regular basis. This makes it more difficult to ignore these ideas. If people can not accept the merits of these ideas or understand why other have these ideas, then they will become more combative and defensive and less willing to compromise. When people are receptive to new ideas and beliefs, then communication is healthy. However, when people are not receptive, then communication can be detrimental when it is forces them to face issues that they are not prepared to face.

If thinking conceptual forces a person to be more receptive to the ideas and beliefs of others, then society should be interested in moving its citizen away from the procedural end of the continuum and toward the conceptual. Being in the middle is the best.

Corporate Cultures

———————— ◆ ————————

Just as individuals have a way of thinking, companies have a way of thinking. This affects the way that they train their employees, how and whom they promote, how they negotiate labor contracts, and how they evolve over time. Most American companies are positioned on the procedural side of the continuum between thinking procedurally and conceptually. There are many reasons why most American companies are procedural. A procedural organization is less likely to recognize changes that may effect its existence. An understanding of why American companies are procedural and why they remain procedural is necessary if they are to be changed.

American business was founded on the military style of management. There were no other large organizations to emulate so it was nature for companies to structure themselves on the same basis. In this type of environment superiors give orders and subordinates follow those orders. There is no opportunity to question the orders. Orders are expected to be followed no matter what the cost. This model worked every well until recent history and has allowed the United States to prosper and grow. However, as business worldwide has become more competitive and complex and the rate of change in technology has increased, this model has lost much of the magic and companies have had to move to a more collaborative environment. Even the military has had to adjust to this new world. Many companies have tried to change their culture to be open, collaborative, and innovative. There are a lot of nice sounding words to define these new types of organizations. Consultants come up with new ones everyday to sell their ideas. However, issuing mission statements, establishing goals, and creating visions with these new words doesn't mean that the corporate culture has changed.

The differences between a traditional organization and an innovative, collaborative one can be summarized in how the organization thinks. Just as an individual needs to understand how he or she thinks, an organization or company needs to understand its mode of thinking. Since most American companies are procedural, most changes or ideas are implemented in American companies as procedures not as ideas. Most management consultants to American companies utilize this even if they don't recognize the fact. When a management consultant has an idea or concept to sell to American companies, they invariably develop a process, procedure, and a series of steps to follow that will change the organization. Processes, procedures, etc. will never change the basic structure of any company in the same way that the personality of an individual can not be changed by making that individual go through a series of steps. Implementing a basic structural change to a person's personality or to the structure of a company is very difficult.

The first step in making a difficult change is awareness and knowledge. People must become aware and accept the current environment and they must gain knowledge about the reasons for and the advantages of change. No person or organization will change if they do not believe that the change will benefit them. Therefore, it is appropriate to analyze some of the indicators of an organization's style of thinking and how it affects their performance.

How an organization trains its employees is an easy way to identify an organization. Training means all types of training not just the training that goes on in a classroom environment. Most training in an organization occurs informally. It occurs when employees change positions within the organization, when superiors give assignments to subordinates, etc. If most of the training and instruction is how to do the job instead of why the job needs to be done, then the organization is thinking procedurally.

Training in American companies is usually directed toward the how and not the why. Most individuals find it more difficult to communicate ideas because it requires more time and effort to document, teach, and test an idea than a process. It is easier to teach the steps in a process and to verify that the student has mastered the steps than it is to explain an idea and to verify that the student has mastered the idea. Therefore, they prefer to communicate procedures. However, if the idea is communicated correctly, then the communication of an idea is easier and faster than the communication of procedures and the students will remember the idea better. When the individuals in the organization only know how to do their jobs, then they will be unable to think in innovative ways about their jobs to propose better and more efficient methods and processes.

As has been discussed before, an idea is much more powerful than a set of procedures or rules. Therefore, a superior may be reluctant to share his or her power with his or her subordinates. It is natural for a person to want to protect their position and stature. Knowledge provides a lot of power and stature to the person who possesses it. They have gain power and prestige within the organization through their knowledge and unless they have a personal incentive to share their knowledge, they will only share that which is least valuable the knowledge of how to do the task.

It is difficult for people to give away their knowledge. They must be convinced that it is in their best interest to do this. Since the benefits accrue to the organization not to the individual, the individuals must be convinced that they must sacrifice their power in order for the organization to continue to prosper and even survive. When the majority of American companies were structured on a hierarchical basis, the status quo was acceptable. However, as many organizations have been threatened with extinction, they have been forced to adjust to the competition. This creates an environment where it is difficult for an organization that does not share knowledge to survive.

Organizations evolve just as living organisms evolve. The evolution of an organization is shaped not by genes but by the individuals and the processes that are used to select the future managers of the organization. Its current management and promotion processes in two ways shape the evolution of an organization. Of course, the most obvious way is by the decisions that management makes about the present and future direction of the company. In addition, they determine the future managers of the company through their decisions on who is promoted and given the opportunity to gain the experience needed to succeed in the future. The problem that faces most organizations is that most managers promote individuals who have similar traits or personalities. Therefore, managers who are procedurally oriented will promote managers who are procedurally oriented. The organization will continue to grow and evolve in the direction that has been established. Only when a new or different perspective is brought into the company can the company start to move in a new direction. This is one reason why most businesses that are in crisis must change their leadership before they are able to make any fundamental changes.

It is important that organizations and people have the ability to perform effectively in both areas of thinking. The most effective organizations are those that excel in both the execution of current procedures and the development of innovative solutions for the future. This is a difficult balance to maintain. The success of some organizations shows that it can be done. In order to maintain a balance the organization must recognize its strengths and weaknesses in the same manner that an individual must recognize them to be able to grow. An organization must also maintain a balance of individuals with different skills. When evaluating an employee for promotion the person's style of thinking should be matched against the requirements of the position. Also, the organization should maintain a balance between procedural and conceptual managers.

One of the biggest obstacles to becoming a conceptual company is the promotion policy of companies. The structure of American society is based on rewarding people for performance. In school people are rewarded for performance on tests. In business they are rewarded for their performance on the job. As they progress through their lives, first as a student and then as they enter their adult life, how their performances are measured changes. When they start out as students or as an employee of a company, they are measured against objective standards. As they progress in these roles, the measures become more subjective and they are expected to be able to more conceptual in nature. There are no rules to follow or the rules are constantly changing. They are less responsible for the specific and more responsible for the general. However, individuals are identified early as future leaders (high performers) not for their conceptual abilities but for their ability to follow specific directions accurately and quickly.

Most promotions in an organization are based on the individual's ability to perform the position that they are currently in not on their ability to perform the position that they are promoted into. The individuals that are able to demonstrate the ability to perform tasks quickly and accurately are the ones that are tracked into the best schools. From the best school they are tracked into the positions in the companies which lead to quick promotions. Therefore, the majority of the people in upper management come from a procedural background. The best of these people have the ability to shift their focus to the concepts as their responsibilities expand. The others remain committed to the procedures and process that have worked in the past.

The fact that most are procedural oriented also leads to the promotion of more procedural oriented people since people tend to promote other people that are like themselves. Therefore, most companies end up with a management structure that can not anticipate or see when fundamental changes are occurring in their industry. When they miss these changes, the consequences can be catastrophic to their companies.

For these reason most companies are procedural in their thinking and continue to be until something dramatic occurs which forces them to change. When a company is forced to change in these situations, the change is never easy and is very difficult. These types of change usually involve a major restructuring which means that employees lose their jobs or benefits and that the owners have lost also. It would be better for a company to implement the changes when they are strong and healthy. However, most companies do not possess a mode of thinking that allows them to recognize the need for change before it is forced on them.

The negotiation of labor contracts is another area where a procedural process has continued even though the basic environment that spawned this process has changed. The American labor movement developed in an environment where American companies had little or no competition from foreign companies. Also, pattern contracts were negotiated so that all of the companies in a given industry were forced to operate under the same contract. These facts led to the negotiation of contracts in bottom up manner with the negotiations being structured as a confrontation. In today's competitive environment where companies, countries, and regions are all competing against each other, the negotiation of a labor contract should be based on a partnership relationship. In a partnership the first issue to be resolve is how the earnings of the partnership are to be divided. In other words how will the pie be divided?

The negotiation of most labor contracts involves the development of agreements on each piece of the contract. These pieces are then combined into an overall contract. The owners or their representatives (Management) have forecasts of revenue that they expect to be generated over the life of the contract. They then base their negotiations on these projections. The union on the other hand is trying to maximize the total economic benefit for their members. In most cases the forecasts for revenue are not discussed with the union because management does not want to share this information.

This process can be compared with the negotiations between business partners. In the negotiations between business partners all parties understand the revenue forecasts. The partners would then discuss how the revenue should be allocated such as reinvestment, benefits, advertising, wages, etc. The decisions are made on a top to bottom basis. This is opposed to the bottom up process that starts with individual agreements on salary and benefits that then have to be fitted into the total cost structure.

Companies and unions talk about becoming partners but they cling to the same old processes. A company that is concept oriented would understand what it means to be partners and change the underlying relationships. When a company is driven by concepts, it does not perpetuate processes that are out of sync with those concepts.

In labor negotiations all of the stakeholders in the company should first come together and agree on how much revenue the company can produce by selling its products or services. Then they must agree on how this revenue will be divided between the stakeholders. This is a top down approach to labor negotiations. This means that all stakeholders must agree on the basic division of revenue. The implementation of these basic decisions will still be the responsibility of the owners of the company and their representatives (management). In actual practice it is not feasible to gather representatives for each class of stakeholders (production workers, management, owners, suppliers, government authorities, etc.) into the room and develop a consensus on the division. However, it is appropriate that labor unions have some input into how the revenue of the company is allocated. For this to work the labor unions must recognize that they are only entitled to a certain portion of the company's revenue which is determined by many factors such as how much risk they are willing to accept, their contribution to the generation of the revenue, etc.

When partners negotiate how earnings will be apportioned, there are various factors which enter into these negotiations such as capital contributed, risk assumed, services provided, etc. This is the opposite of labor negotiation where wages, benefits, etc. are negotiated separately. The costs are then summed up to a total that represents a percentage of the revenue of the company. When negotiations are based on a percentage of revenue, then wages, benefits, etc. are added to the contract until the total reaches the amount allocated to labor from the company's total revenue. Any organization where one individual or a group of individuals take too large a share of the organization's revenue is headed for trouble. When the current process was developed, the relationships between the various groups in the organization could be maintained because all of the competitive organizations were operating under the same rules. Under the old set of rules after the contract was negotiated, the price of the product was set to recuperate the cost. This worked when all companies were operating under the same conditions but now the cost structures for different companies are substantially different. Since the rules have changed, the process needs to change.

The fact that the majority of American companies have a style of thinking that is weighed toward the procedural side has several implications. A procedural organization is less likely to recognize a change that will fundamentally alter the market that they compete in (a paradigm shift). The change may involve customer expectations, new technology, etc. The organizations that are best able to identify these changes will prosper and will evolve smoothly to operate in the new environments. Those who don't recognize these changes will either perish or will be forced to make fundamental changes when their survival is in question. Change is always stressful. However, to be forced to change when the organization is failing, your competitors are growing, etc. is more stress that any organization or individual should have to endure. Companies need to change their mode of thinking to be more conceptually driven.

Education

◆

The system of formal education that has been implemented in the United States is geared toward procedural excellence. Most of the educational yardsticks that are used today measure the ability of schools to teach rules and procedures that can be qualified and objectively evaluated. Since the measurement of conceptual understanding is more difficult to measure and evaluate, it is natural that school and colleges will move toward this. People feel better knowing that they are teaching something that can be measured. People know that they are getting their money worth because they can measure the results.

The evaluation of the education process is important. Schools and colleges should be held accountable for producing students that can perform in society. Society needs individuals that can follow rules and learn new procedures. However, society also needs individuals who are capable of recognizing and understanding the changes that are occurring in the world. Individuals who are able to adjust to the dynamics of a world that are evolving at an exponential rate. If a society is to continue to thrive, then that society needs to insure that every individual has the opportunity to utilize his or her abilities to the maximum. A person that does not understand his or her strengths and weaknesses will never be able to fully utilize them.

School can and should encourage students to understand and explore their strengths and weaknesses. Every student should be recognize for their strengths and encouraged to work on the areas that are weak. Remember the most successful individuals are those who can most able to adapt to different situations. Therefore, schools and colleges should evaluate how students think. There is a danger when any type of label is applied to an individual but sometimes it is necessary. The positives exceed the negatives. Students that learn procedural could be matched with teachers that are teach procedural or special assistance could be provided when the thinking style of the teacher and the student clash.

If society benefits the most from the population which is well rounded and moderate (neither all procedural or all conceptual but most individuals are able to do both), then one goal of education should be to identify the thinking style of the students and increase their tolerance for thinking in a different way. Just as school should not try to replace the moral values that the student's parent give them but teach the student to understand and respect the moral values of others, a student's way of thinking should not be changed. However, the student should be able to understand the differences and recognize the values and virtues of each. They should be given the opportunity to utilize and master both.

Everyone needs to feel good about themselves. If the educational system recognizes the value of the different style of thinking, then students will understand why they may be having difficulty in a particular class and not another class. Understanding why is the first step to correcting the problem. Problem may be the teaching style of the instructor. Therefore, a change to a new teacher may be appropriate or the services of a tutor who can bridge the differences between the thinking style of the teacher and the student may be necessary.

The formal education process needs to be more flexible. It has to recognize the differences in the thinking styles of students and should encourage these differences. This will be very difficult since the educational system is faced with many other priorities and problems that also demand time and money.

Society

———————— ◆ ————————

Today's era is very dynamic. Society is experiencing a rate of change that is astounding. These changes are affecting all areas of people's lives (work, leisure, education, etc.). This necessitates a greater degree of specialization. As the amount of information expands, the need for specialists increases. Specialization allows individuals to demand more for their services because when expertise is needed, only they have the required knowledge and experience. However, there is a negative to this specialization. The negative is that change may make this expertise obsolete or worthless. Therefore, it is important to society and to the individuals that these specialists be able to understand and recognize the paradigm shift that will render their expertise obsolete. This will require that ability to think conceptually whereas the specialist was very procedural oriented.

Since the most institutions and individuals in a society are procedural oriented, societies are inclined to be procedural oriented. This has its advantages and its disadvantages. Just as there are advantages and disadvantages for an individual or institution.

The reader might not believe that the difference in how people think would have any effect on their personal relationships. However, it effects their personal relationships in two ways. When a person communicates with other individuals, their style of thinking will control what information they communicate and how the other person will receive what is said. Therefore, it is important to understand any differences to insure a clear line of communication. Clear communications are important between individuals as well as between organizations or countries. When people are not communicating in the same style, then the tendency is to not listen. People are conditioned to ignore information and data that is not relevant to them. A communication that is not in sync with their internal mode of thinking is more likely to be ignored. It is important to understand this type of behavior so that communications can be tailored to the audience. People who are members of an audience need to make a more conscious effort to listen when the message does not fit their style of thinking.

The second way that people's style of thinking effects their relationships is that a procedural person is less likely to analyze the behavior of others that a conceptual person. When someone is passed on the highway, do they consider why the person is driving fast? Do they ever consider that the person might be on the way to the hospital? They are less likely to get upset with another person if they think about why the other person may be acting in a certain way than if they only think about the other person's actions. Just the time and effect that it takes to think about the motives of others will give people time to calm down and consider any actions on their part. In a modern society where the pressures and problems that everyone seems to face increase daily, it is important that people see others with the same problems and concerns that they have. This will increase people's tolerance of others. Hopefully, this discussion has convinced the reader that people's general attitude toward thinking will have an effect on their relationships with others.

Conclusion

———————◆———————

If this book has given the reader some entertainment and mostly if it has caused the reader to evaluate their thinking style, then it has been successful. There is a short test in Appendix A if the reader has not been able to identify their thinking style or they would like to confirm their thinking style. This understanding will hopefully allow the reader to function better and understand why they think as they do and why they have difficulty in communicating with others sometimes.

Being a procedural person is not better than being a conceptual person or vice versa. What is important is that people understand themselves and maximize their personal potential. It is also important that society use this knowledge to develop a better future for everyone.

Appendix A

◆

Thinking Style Test

Mark each question with a number from 1 to 10. 1 = very strongly disagree 10 = very strongly agree

1. I am satisfied to understand the rules and don't need to know why. _____
2. I am very detail oriented. _____
3. I like highly structured work. _____
4. I enjoy being an expert in a specific subject. _____
5. Change is very stressful. _____
6. I become bored quickly with new work or educational assignments. _____
7. I create detail instructions for performing tasks (new recipes, work tasks, etc.). _____
8. I take lots of notes when learning something new. _____

The higher the score on this simple test, then the more likely the person is procedurally oriented and a lower score would indicate a more concept-oriented person.

www.ingramcontent.com/pod-product-compliance
Lightning Source LLC
Chambersburg PA
CBHW030900180526
45163CB00004B/1641